Discovery. The purpose is for *you* to interact with John's Gospel. "Questions for Careful Reading" is a tool to help you dig into the text and examine it carefully. "Questions for Application" will help you consider what John's words mean for your life here and now. Each week concludes with an "Approach to Prayer" section that helps you respond to God's word. Supplementary "Living Tradition" and "Saints in the Making" sections offer the thoughts and experiences of Christians past and present in order to show you what the Gospel of John has meant to others—so that you can consider what it might mean for you.

How long are the discussion sessions? We've assumed you will have about an hour and a half when you get together. If you have less time, you'll find that most of the elements can be shortened somewhat.

Is homework necessary? You will get the most out of your discussions if you read the weekly material and prepare your answers to the questions in advance of each meeting. But if participants are not able to prepare, have someone read the "What's Happened" and "Guide to the Reading" sections aloud to the group at the points where they occur in the weekly material.

What about leadership? If you happen to have a world-class biblical scholar in your group, by all means ask him or her to lead the discussions. But in the absence of any professional Scripture scholars, or even accomplished biblical amateurs, you can still have a first-class Bible discussion. Choose two or three people to be facilitators, and have everyone read "Suggestions for Bible Discussion Groups" (page 92) before beginning.

Does everyone need a guide? a Bible? Everyone in the group will need their own copy of this booklet. It contains the sections of John that are discussed, so a Bible is not absolutely necessary—but each participant will find it useful to have one. You should have at least one Bible on hand for your discussion. (See page 96 for recommendations.)

How do we get started? Before you begin, take a look at the suggestions for Bible discussion groups (page 92) or individuals (page 95).

John 11–21: A Story Simple Yet Profound

Beginning to read the Gospel of John at chapter 11 is like putting the second tape of a two-part movie into the video-cassette player first. You've missed half the story! Reading the first ten chapters of John is obviously the preferred way to get to chapter 11. But John's Gospel is not a murder mystery with a convoluted plot. With a little catching up, you can follow the second half without necessarily having read the first half. So let me give you a brief rundown on what has happened. (Another Six Weeks with the Bible booklet, *John 1–10: I Am the Bread of Life,* provides an introduction to the first ten chapters of the Gospel of John.)

The story line of John's Gospel is actually quite simple. God has come into the world in the person of Jesus of Nazareth. To be precise, Jesus is God's "Word"—he is one with God while being somehow distinct from God. John states this mysterious truth in the first seventeen verses of his Gospel. If you don't have time to read all of chapters 1 through 10, try at least to read 1:1–17 (unless otherwise indicated, all biblical citations in this booklet are from the Gospel of John).

John skips over Jesus' birth and early years, opening his account when Jesus is already a man. Jesus teaches, performs symbolic actions, like clearing merchants out of the Jerusalem temple, and demonstrates a remarkable power over nature by performing acts such as changing water to wine for a wedding celebration and curing blindness and other afflictions. Jesus presents a sharply focused message: "I am God's unique, personal representative to the human race. I am fully authorized to act on God's behalf because I am and have always been one with God." Jesus expresses his union with God by calling God "my Father" and referring to himself as "the Son."

Unlike the other Gospels, in which Jesus offers substantial teaching about how to live, in John's Gospel Jesus' preaching is focused mainly on proclaiming his identity and calling people to believe in him. He summons people to recognize who he is and to enter a personal relationship with him so that they can receive the divine life that he offers.

JOHN 11–21

My Peace
I Give You

A Guided Discovery for Groups and Individuals

Kevin Perrotta

LOYOLAPRESS.

CHICAGO

LOYOLAPRESS.

3441 N. ASHLAND AVENUE
CHICAGO, ILLINOIS 60657
(800) 621-1008
WWW.LOYOLABOOKS.ORG

Imprimatur	*Nihil Obstat*
Most Reverend Raymond E. Goedert,	Reverend John Lodge, S.S.L., S.T.D.
M.A., S.T.L., J.C.L.	Censor Deputatus
Vicar General	July 12, 2001
Archdiocese of Chicago	
July 23, 2001	

The *Nihil Obstat* and *Imprimatur* are official declarations that a book is free of doctrinal and moral error. No implication is contained therein that those who have granted the *Nihil Obstat* and *Imprimatur* agree with the content, opinions, or statements expressed.

The Scripture quotations contained herein are from the New Revised Standard Version Bible: Catholic Edition, copyright © 1993 and 1989 by the Division of Christian Education of the National Council of the Churches of Christ in the U.S.A. Used by permission. All rights reserved. Subheadings in Scripture quotations have been added by the author.

The reflections by St. Augustine (p. 22) are from *In Johannis Evangelium*, Corpus Christianorum, Series Latina, vol. 36 (Turnholt, Belgium: Typographi Brepols Editores Pontificii, 1954), Tractatus 49, 419–33. Translation by Kevin Perrotta. An English version may be found in John W. Rettig, trans., *Tractates on the Gospel of John*, The Fathers of the Church, vols. 78, 79, 88, 90, 92 (New York: Fathers of the Church, Inc., 1988–95).

The excerpt from John Henry Newman (p. 23) is from *Parochial and Plain Sermons*, vol. 3, sermon 10, which can be viewed at www.newmanreader.org.

The Greek text of John Chrysostom's homilies on John (p. 35) can be found in *Patrologia Graeca*, vol. 59, col. 371, edited by J.-P. Migne. Translation by Kevin Perrotta. An English version may be found in Sister Thomas Aquinas Goggin, trans., *Commentary on Saint John the Apostle and Evangelist: Homilies 1–88*, The Fathers of the Church, vols. 33, 41 (New York: Fathers of the Church, Inc., 1957, 1960).

The reflections from Thérèse of Lisieux (pp. 47, 72), are from *L'oeuvre complète de Sainte Thérèse de l'Enfant-Jésus: Manuscrits autobiographiques ("Histoire d'une âme")* (Paris: Editions du Cerf, 1997). Translation by Louise M. Perrotta. An English version may be found in *The Story of a Soul*, trans. Michael Day (Westminster, Md.: Newman Press, 1952), 66–67, 146–47.

The meditation by William S. Kurz, S.J. (p. 58) is from *Farewell Addresses in the New Testament* (Collegeville, Minn.: The Liturgical Press, 1990), 89–90.

The story of Bob Mitchell (p. 59) appeared, in a different form, in the July 1998 issue of *God's Word Today* magazine (P.O. Box 56915, Boulder, CO 80323).

The prayer by Caryll Houselander (p. 71) is from *The Way of the Cross* (New York: Sheed & Ward, 1955), 129–30. Reprinted by permission of Sheed & Ward, an Apostolate of the Priests of the Sacred Heart, 7373 S. Lovers Lane Road, Franklin, WI 53132.

The prayer by John Henry Newman (p. 82) is from "Meditations on Christian Doctrine" in *Meditations and Devotions* (London: Longman, Green, and Company, 1953), 198–99.

The Odes of Solomon (p. 90), Syriac text with an English translation, can be found in James H. Charlesworth, ed. and trans., *The Odes of Solomon: The Syriac Texts* (Missoula, Mont.: Scholars Press, 1977), 137–43. Translation by Kevin Perrotta.

Interior design by Kay Hartmann/Communique Design
Illustration by Charise Mericle Harper

ISBN 0-8294-1569-6

Printed in the United States of America
05 06 07 08 09 10 Bang 9 8 7 6 5 4

Contents

How to Use This Guide

You might compare the Bible to a national park. The park is so large that you could spend months, even years, getting to know it. But a brief visit, if carefully planned, can be enjoyable and worthwhile. In a few hours you can drive through the park and pull over at a handful of sites. At each stop you can get out of the car, take a short trail through the woods, listen to the wind blowing in the trees, get a feel for the place.

In this booklet we'll drive through a small portion of the Bible—the second half of John's Gospel—making half a dozen stops along the way. At those points we'll proceed on foot, taking a leisurely walk through the selected passages. The readings have been chosen to take us to the heart of John's portrayal of Jesus. After each discussion we'll get back in the car and take the highway to the next stop. "Between Discussions" pages summarize the portions of the Gospel that we will pass by.

This guide provides everything you need to begin exploring John, chapters 11 through 21, in six discussions—or to do a six-part exploration on your own. The introduction on page 6 will prepare you to get the most out of your reading. The weekly sections feature key passages from the Gospel, with explanations that highlight what these words mean for us today. Equally important, each section supplies questions that will launch you into fruitful discussion, helping you to both explore the Gospel for yourself and learn from one another. If you're using the booklet by yourself, the questions will spur your personal reflection.

Each discussion is meant to be a *guided discovery*.

Guided. None of us is equipped to read the Bible without help. We read the Bible *for* ourselves but not *by* ourselves. Scripture was written to be understood and applied in the community of faith. So each week "A Guide to the Reading," drawing on the work of both modern biblical scholars and Christian writers of the past, supplies background and explanations. The guide will help you grasp the message of John's Gospel. Think of it as a friendly park ranger who points out noteworthy details and explains what you're looking at so you can appreciate things for yourself.

Jesus is a Jew, as are the people he addresses. By his preaching, symbolic acts, and miracles he announces that he is the climax of God's dealings with the Jewish people. While many of his fellow Jews are inclined to welcome him (how well they understand him is open to question), most of the leaders are not. As Jesus carries on his ministry, the leaders become increasingly hostile. Jesus drops hints that he expects to meet a violent death. At the point where we pick up the story, in chapter 11, there has just been an attempt on his life in Jerusalem, and he has withdrawn from the city for safety.

Just as the story up through chapter 10 can be summarized simply, so can the remainder of John's Gospel. Jesus will now provide the most impressive sign of his divine origin (our reading in Week 1) and will bring his public ministry to a close (Week 2). After giving his disciples final instructions (Weeks 3 and 4), he will accept an agonizing death and will rise from the dead (Weeks 5 and 6). Like the swing of a pendulum, the Gospel of John has two complementary movements: the Word of God enters the world as Jesus of Nazareth; then, for the sake of human beings, he leaves the world and returns to God.

Most of us are not very interested in discussing the meanings of words. We all know the frustration of reaching the end of such discussions more confused than when we began. But one term in John's Gospel is so central to his meaning, yet so complex and elusive, that it is worth taking a few minutes to investigate it. If we can get hold of this word, it will lead us to the heart of John's understanding of Jesus. The word is *glory*.

Glory has a special meaning in John's Gospel. Here are some verses in our target readings that speak of *glory*:

◆ "Did I not tell you that if you believed, you would see the glory of God?" (11:40).

◆ "His disciples did not understand these things at first; but when Jesus was glorified, then they remembered that these things had been written of him" (12:16).

◆ "The hour has come for the Son of Man to be glorified" (12:23).

- "Father, glorify your name." . . . "I have glorified it, and I will glorify it again" (12:28).
- "Now the Son of Man has been glorified, and God has been glorified in him. If God has been glorified in him, God will also glorify him in himself and will glorify him at once" (13:31–32).

As we all know, the English word *glory* has various meanings. It denotes splendor and magnificence ("She was struck by the glory of the scene, the sun glinting on the lake and the spruce forest giving off a pungent fragrance"). It also denotes the social recognition given to what is splendid and magnificent ("In pursuing a political career he was motivated by a concern for national welfare rather than a desire for personal glory"). To *glorify* is to bestow honor and praise on that which is splendid and magnificent.

With these ordinary meanings in mind, we can begin to grasp what Jesus means in the first passage above (11:40). He tells Martha, the sister of Lazarus, that she will "see the glory of God." Jesus is about to raise her brother from the grave, and this will display God's magnificent, life-giving power.

Once we know the context, we can also understand what John means when he writes of the time after Jesus was "glorified" (12:16). John is speaking about the period after Jesus' resurrection, when he has returned to the condition of heavenly splendor that was his as the Word of God from before all time.

But the remaining passages quoted above are more difficult to decipher. What does it mean, for example, that God has been "glorified" in the Son (13:31)?

To understand these passages we need to look back to the Old Testament. It is here that the people of Israel pondered on the God who had revealed himself to them. As creator, they realized, God is splendid and magnificent, deserving praise and honor. God has glory and deserves glory. But the most glorious thing about God, it seemed to the Israelites, was the way he repeatedly came to their assistance and showed them his kindness in real-life situations. From their experience of him, the Israelites learned that God's mercy is as great as his majesty (Exodus 33:19; Sirach 2:18). It became clear to them that God displays his grandeur not only through the splendor of creation but also through acts of justice and compassion.

Thus the psalmists equated God's glory with his "steadfast love" (Psalms 57:5, 10; 63:2–3). They praised God for showing his glory by rescuing the downtrodden, doing "wondrous works" for the suffering, and saving people in distress (Psalms 72:18–19; 85:9–10; 96:3; 102:15–17; 108:5–6; 138:5–6). The Israelites spoke of God glorifying himself by saving people from evil and filling their lives with blessing. Of course, people do naturally glorify God when he demonstrates his kindness to them.

These thoughts lie in the background of John's Gospel. In the Gospel, *glory* and *glorify* refer to God showing his love. When John writes that the Word of God has come into the world to glorify God, he means that the Word has come to express God's love by rescuing us from the sources of our unhappiness, leading us to love and praise God in return. Jesus directs his whole life toward the moment when he will glorify God completely by his death. "It is for this reason that I have come," Jesus declares, and immediately prays, "Father, glorify your name" (12:27–28). Jesus' death will be God's supreme wondrous work. In his dying, Jesus will bring God's love to bear in the most profound way to uproot the evils that afflict us. He will root out sin, death, and the Devil—the evils that destroy our personalities, our relationships, our very lives.

John's use of *glory* and *glorify* brings us face-to-face with an apparent contradiction. To identify the agony and shame of crucifixion with *glory* seems to stretch the word beyond the breaking point. Jesus' crucifixion must have appeared to witnesses as an unspeakably degrading death, as the exact opposite of *glory*. Yet Jesus sees—and wishes us to see—something splendid and magnificent in his death. What could that be?

The glory of the cross is a paradox too profound for any simple explanation, and each of us must ponder it for ourselves. But one line of thinking is this: God and Jesus were *glorified* at the cross because Jesus' death was God's supreme revelation of himself. At the cross God reveals himself as a loving Father who gives what is most precious—his own Son—to the world. He also reveals

9

himself as a loving Son who, through suffering, gives his whole life back to the Father for the world. God is glorified at the cross because he shows forth the splendor and magnificence of his love. To the ordinary eye, Jesus hanging on the cross appears to be an image of shame and defeat. Yet if our eyes could see love as light, we would find the cross intensely bright; looking at the cross would be as blinding as staring at the sun. By the language of glory, John opens our eyes to this invisible radiance at Golgotha. He helps us to see what most of those present at the crucifixion could not see: the love of Father and Son for one another and for the human race.

God and Jesus are glorified, or revealed, at the cross, yet the cross is a dark glory, a hidden revelation. And this paradox continues in our lives. Jesus has now risen from death to life, but his triumph is not manifested publicly to the world. He reveals himself to his disciples who believe in him, not to the world that does not believe (14:19). The power of evil is broken (12:31), yet not driven out, as every day's newspapers and news reports remind us. Having risen from death, Jesus gives divine life here and now, the life that overcomes death. Yet each of us will die. We must still look forward to a final day when Jesus will raise us up into life, physically and spiritually, once and for all. John writes his Gospel to help us perceive and live in this paradox. The great mystery of the cross—the central fact of our faith—is captured in the paradoxical word *glory*. Keep this in mind as you read John's Gospel.

John's Gospel is also the great revelation of the Holy Spirit. John helps us to see Jesus as the revelation of God and to accept the gift of life that comes through his death and resurrection. If we are really to see and know and live, however, we need more than a book; we need God to reveal himself to us in a living, personal way. This is where the third divine person comes in—the Holy Spirit. In a lengthy after-dinner talk on the eve of his death, Jesus assures his disciples that his departure will greatly benefit them, for it will make possible the coming of the Spirit. Jesus characterizes the Spirit as "another Advocate"—that is, another person like himself, Jesus being the first Advocate.

Through the coming of the Spirit, Jesus and the Father will live within the disciples. Because of the Spirit, a personal relationship with Jesus, through which he shares the life of God with us, will not be merely an idea we read about in a book but a direct experience, even for us who live centuries after Jesus' earthly life.

Knowing when, where, and for whom a book was written often helps us understand it. Unfortunately, scholars are far from agreeing about the date, origin, and original audience of John's Gospel. Most scholars, however, tend to think that John's Gospel, completed perhaps in the nineties of the first century, was the last of the four Gospels to be written.

The question of who wrote the Gospel of John might at first seem to have an obvious answer: John wrote it. But then, who was John? In our target readings we meet an unnamed "disciple whom Jesus loved" (13:23; 19:26; 21:7), who seems to have been the source of the tradition about Jesus that is presented in the Gospel (19:35; 21:24). Traditionally, this "beloved disciple" has been identified with the apostle John, one of the sons of Zebedee, mentioned in the other Gospels (Matthew 4:21). But scholars find reasons to question this identification. In addition, scholars disagree about the specific role that this "beloved disciple" played in the formation of the Gospel as we have it. Did he write it? Did he write parts of it? Did he convey the tradition about Jesus that is reflected in the Gospel, while leaving the writing to others? All these views have found scholarly defenders.

Happily, we do not have to answer these questions in order to benefit from the Gospel. Whoever the "beloved disciple" was, and whatever part he played in composing the Gospel, the finished product rests on his testimony. Thus the Gospel conveys the testimony of a companion of Jesus, shaped by many years of Spirit-guided prayer and reflection. By including this Gospel in its authoritative collection of books—the New Testament—the Church has indicated its recognition that this Gospel gives authentic testimony to Jesus. While acknowledging the questions about the authorship—and editorship—of the Gospel, in this booklet we will simply refer to the author as John.

A further point concerning the "disciple whom Jesus loved" is worth noting. His anonymity makes it easy for us to put ourselves in his place as we read. The beloved disciple is a kind of blank into which each of us can fill in our own name. When we read of this disciple reclining next to Jesus at the Last Supper, we can enter the event by picturing ourselves in his place. When we read of the beloved disciple standing at the cross, we can imagine that we are that disciple, watching Jesus as he dies and listening to what he says. This is no reader's trick. Each of us *is* the disciple whom Jesus loves.

Advice for reading. As I said earlier, John's Gospel is not a suspense story. John wrote for Christians, who already knew how the story turned out. His Gospel is rather a drama, with striking contrasts, dizzying paradoxes, and tragic ironies. A suspense story is best the first time you read it. A good drama gets better with every reading, for it discloses its depths only as we reread it.

John's Gospel is deceptively simple. The author loads little everyday words with a heavy freight of meaning. A single gesture or phrase may allude to a passage in the Old Testament, thus drawing into the narrative an entire prophecy or prefigurement. Once you get a feel for the depth and complexity of John's seemingly simple account, you begin to examine every word and sentence carefully, listening for resonances of meaning that you may not have heard at first.

John's Gospel is instant mental overload. We cannot absorb the whole message with one reading. The Gospel is not a glass of water to drink down but a sea to swim in. We can never entirely plumb its depths. But as we read and reread, we will grow in understanding. Along the way, we should feel free to stop at any point to ponder any word or statement that seems to have personal significance.

Before we begin, a word is in order about John's references to the Jews. Almost everyone in the Gospel account is Jewish, but, for complex reasons, John usually uses the term "the Jews" to refer only to some Jews, specifically to those Jews who did not accept Jesus, especially the Jewish leaders. The fact that these people who rejected him were Jews is, of course, a reflection of the actual history. Many of the Jewish people who heard and saw Jesus did not accept his claims about himself, and some of the leaders played a part in having him put to death. John's practice of referring to these people simply as "the Jews" has a complicated historical background that cannot be unraveled here. What is important to note is that in his drama, John lets those Jews who rejected Jesus stand as representatives of the whole of human society. They represent all of us, to the extent that we do not fully grasp and wholeheartedly respond to Jesus. Their refusal to believe in Jesus did not stem from their Jewishness, but from their commitment to interests that ran counter to God's plan: for some, a desire for social acceptance, an unwillingness to let go of political and religious prerogatives. These, of course, are our faults too.

It is a mistake to read John's negative characterizations of "the Jews" as an actual description of all Jews even at the time of Jesus. It is an even bigger mistake to use his negative view of "the Jews" as a pretext for any sort of negative view of Jewish people in the past or present—a mistake that sadly has often been made. To avoid this misunderstanding, some scholars have adopted the practice of putting quotation marks around "the Jews" in their discussions of John's Gospel. This serves as a reminder that John uses the term with a special meaning—to refer to those Jewish leaders and people who rejected Jesus as representatives of the world that rejects him. The bishops of the Second Vatican Council (1962–65) as well as Pope John Paul II have condemned anti-Semitism in all its forms.

WAKE UP, MY FRIEND

Questions to Begin

15 minutes
Use a question or two to get warmed up for the reading.

1 When was the last time you got a phone call or letter from someone you know asking for help? What was the problem? What did you do?

2 How do you wake up?
❑ Very slowly.
❑ Gradually, with coffee.
❑ Early. I like the morning.
❑ Very early, without an alarm, and ready to take on the world.

3 What is the worst stench you have ever smelled? (No bathroom odors, please!)

5 minutes
Read the passage aloud. Let individuals take turns reading
paragraphs.

The Reading: John 11:1–44

An Urgent Message

1 Now a certain man was ill, Lazarus of Bethany, the village of Mary and her sister Martha. 2 Mary was the one who anointed the Lord with perfume . . . her brother Lazarus was ill. 3 So the sisters sent a message to Jesus, "Lord, he whom you love is ill." 4 But when Jesus heard it, he said, "This illness does not lead to death; rather it is for God's glory, so that the Son of God may be glorified through it." 5 Accordingly, though Jesus loved Martha and her sister and Lazarus, 6 after having heard that Lazarus was ill, he stayed two days longer in the place where he was.

7 Then after this he said to the disciples, "Let us go to Judea again." 8 The disciples said to him, "Rabbi, the Jews were just now trying to stone you, and are you going there again?" 9 Jesus answered, "Are there not twelve hours of daylight? Those who walk during the day do not stumble, because they see the light of this world. . . ." 11 After saying this, he told them, "Our friend Lazarus has fallen asleep, but I am going there to awaken him." 12 The disciples said to him, "Lord, if he has fallen asleep, he will be all right." 13 Jesus, however, had been speaking about his death, but they thought that he was referring merely to sleep. 14 Then Jesus told them plainly, "Lazarus is dead. 15 For your sake I am glad I was not there, so that you may believe. But let us go to him." 16 Thomas, who was called the Twin, said to his fellow disciples, "Let us also go, that we may die with him."

A Scene of Grief

17 When Jesus arrived, he found that Lazarus had already been in the tomb four days. 18 Now Bethany was near Jerusalem, some two miles away, 19 and many of the Jews had come to Martha and Mary to console them about their brother. When Martha heard that Jesus was coming, she went and met him, while Mary stayed at home. 21 Martha said to Jesus, "Lord, if you had been here, my brother would not have died. 22 But even now I know that God will give you whatever you ask of him." 23 Jesus said to her, "Your brother will rise again." 24 Martha said to him, "I know that he will rise again in the resurrection on the last day." 25 Jesus said to her, "I am the resurrection and the life.

Those who believe in me, even though they die, will live, 26 and everyone who lives and believes in me will never die. Do you believe this?" 27 She said to him, "Yes, Lord, I believe that you are the Messiah, the Son of God, the one coming into the world."

28 When she had said this, she went back and called her sister Mary, and told her privately, "The Teacher is here and is calling for you." 29 And when she heard it, she got up quickly and went to him. . . . 31 The Jews who were with her in the house, consoling her, . . . followed her because they thought that she was going to the tomb to weep there. 32 When Mary came where Jesus was and saw him, she knelt at his feet and said to him, "Lord, if you had been here, my brother would not have died." 33 When Jesus saw her weeping, and the Jews who came with her also weeping, he was greatly disturbed in spirit and deeply moved. 34 He said, "Where have you laid him?" They said to him, "Lord, come and see." 35 Jesus began to weep. 36 So the Jews said, "See how he loved him!" 37 But some of them said, "Could not he who opened the eyes of the blind man have kept this man from dying?"

A Life-Giving Command

38 Then Jesus, again greatly disturbed, came to the tomb. It was a cave, and a stone was lying against it. 39 Jesus said, "Take away the stone." Martha, the sister of the dead man, said to him, "Lord, already there is a stench because he has been dead four days." 40 Jesus said to her, "Did I not tell you that if you believed, you would see the glory of God?" 41 So they took away the stone. And Jesus looked upward and said, "Father, I thank you for having heard me. 42 I knew that you always hear me, but I have said this for the sake of the crowd standing here, so that they may believe that you sent me." 43 When he had said this, he cried with a loud voice, "Lazarus, come out!" 44 The dead man came out, his hands and feet bound with strips of cloth, and his face wrapped in a cloth. Jesus said to them, "Unbind him, and let him go."

10 minutes
Choose questions according to your interest and time.

1   If Jesus had left for Bethany as soon as he heard of Lazarus's illness, could he have arrived before his death? (Consider the data in 11:6, 17.) Would Jesus have known this? (Consider 11:4, 11, 14–15.) Why do you suppose he took his time?

2   Why does Jesus describe Lazarus as being "asleep" (11:11)? (Compare similar misunderstandings: 3:3–8; 4:10–14; 7:33–36; 8:21–24.)

3   Is Thomas expressing faith in verse 16?

4   From Jesus' own words throughout this episode, what seems to be his chief concern?

5   Reread verses 25 to 27. Does Martha believe that Jesus is what he says he is? (Take 11:39 into account.)

6   Jesus prays aloud (11:41–42), apparently to keep the bystanders from reaching a wrong conclusion. What misunderstanding is he trying to avoid?

A Guide to the Reading

If participants have not read this section already, read it aloud.
Otherwise go on to "Questions for Application."

The sight of Lazarus emerging from the doorway of the tomb grips the imagination. But stripped of its meaning, the event would remain a mere *X-Files* curiosity. Wanting us to grasp its significance, John devotes most of his narrative not to the act of resuscitation but to the interaction between Jesus and the people around him. The dialogue highlights the issue of Jesus' identity. The drama lies not only in the question "What will Jesus do for Lazarus?" but also in the questions "Who is Jesus?" and "Will anyone recognize him for who he is?"

Verses 5 and 6 are puzzling. Presumably Jesus knows that it is too late to reach Lazarus before he dies, yet he decides to arrive four days after his death rather than two, perhaps to make the raising a more stunning demonstration of his life-giving power (11:14–15).

Jesus seems to operate with a different agenda from the people around him. He does not share their preoccupation with Lazarus's fate. While he loves Lazarus, he seems mainly concerned with people's faith in himself (11:14–15, 25–26, 40, 41–42). Apparently, even after following him for a couple of years, his disciples have not attained complete faith in him (11:15).

Jesus says that the one who believes in him will go on living forever (11:25–26), because the believer in him has already entered into everlasting life, a life that death cannot destroy. For such a person, death is not annihilation, but a door that leads to greater life. Jesus says that he *is* the resurrection: he is the source of divine life here and now, as well as the agent of full resurrection in the future (he has already spoken of giving life both now and in the future—5:24–25).

Martha works from a Jewish expectation that God will raise the dead at the end of time (11:24). She does not realize, however, that with Jesus' arrival the last times have begun. The person speaking to her is the Resurrection in person. Martha comes close to the truth about Jesus (11:27). Yet she does not exactly affirm what Jesus declares of himself (compare 11:25–26 with 11:27). Her reaction to the idea of opening the tomb (11:39) shows the limit of her faith. (Compare Jesus' mother's attitude—2:5.)

The crowd fails to grasp that Jesus not only *could* have saved Lazarus from death (11:37), he can restore him to life. Not even Martha's sister Mary seems to fully believe (11:32).

Thus as Jesus approaches Lazarus's tomb, he may experience not only sorrow (11:35) but anger (11:33, 38). The Greek of verse 33 conveys disapproval; it can be translated, "He became angry in spirit" or "moved with indignation." Biblical scholar Ben Witherington III comments: "Since we are told that what sparks this reaction in Jesus is the weeping of Mary and the Jews, the most natural conclusion is that Jesus is upset at their lack of faith, for they mourned as people without hope for Lazarus's immediate future, while they were in the presence of One who was both resurrection and life." Another scholar, Francis J. Maloney, S.D.B., writes, "As Jesus' public ministry draws to a close he is frustrated and angrily disappointed. . . . Will no one come to belief?" Thus Jesus weeps not only for Lazarus but for those around him, none of whom yet understands who he is. We may even detect in his words to Martha (11:40) a note of irritation—the kind a parent might feel who cannot find any way to overcome a child's conviction that he or she is not loved.

By raising Lazarus, Jesus confirms his claim to be the resurrection. He glorifies God (11:40), that is, he reveals God's life-giving power. And raising Lazarus will glorify God in a further way: it will provoke the religious leaders to decide to have Jesus killed (11:45–53), and by his death Jesus will glorify God by fully demonstrating God's self-giving love. The cross will demonstrate that God is a Father of infinite mercy who gives what is most precious to him—his own Son—for the life of the world (3:16).

Jesus knows he will pay with his life for restoring Lazarus. At Bethany, then, Jesus decides to lay down his life for his friend. The riveting image of Lazarus recalled to life, standing in the doorway of his tomb, is a key for interpreting Jesus' death: he will die in order to give life to his friends. He will die for us, the Lazaruses of the world.

Questions for Application

40 minutes
Choose questions according to your interest and time.

1   When have you discovered that Jesus' agenda or timing for your life is different from your own? How has this affected your relationship with him?

2   Why does Jesus ask Martha the question in verse 26? How would you answer his question?

3   What does Jesus' manner of relating to his followers in this incident tell us about how he relates to us when our faith in him is weak and imperfect?

4   This is the only passage in John's Gospel in which Jesus weeps (11:35). How do you react to his tears? What significance for your relationship with Jesus do you find in his reactions in verses 33, 35, and 38?

5 How does faith in Jesus' words in verses 25 and 26 affect a person's grief over the death of loved ones? How does grief affect a person's faith in Jesus? How does this passage affect how you look at the death of those you love?

6 Has anyone recently let you know that they need your help or presence as they go through a difficult time? How should you respond?

Make personal, honest applications and commit yourself to letting God's word change you.

Whitney Kuniholm, *John: The Living Word,* A Fisherman Bible Study Guide

Approach to Prayer

15 minutes
Use this approach—or create your own!

◆ Read aloud these thoughts of St. Augustine. After silent reflection, pray together, "Lord, have mercy!" and conclude with the Our Father.

A person who has become accustomed to sinning has not only died but is buried, pressed down by the massive weight of habit. How many of us are oppressed by a heavy mass of bad habits! If someone says, "Don't do this. It will destroy you," they answer, "We can't get free of it." How hard it is for one weighed down by bad habits to rise up. But nevertheless we *do* rise up, because we receive life by hidden, inner grace. Jesus shouted, "Lazarus, come out!" and immediately the dead man came forth. Thus every day we see people living well whose worst habits have been completely changed. It is written for every person weighed down by a bad habit that Jesus "came to the tomb."

Jesus Wept

This section is a supplement for individual reading.

F rom a sermon by John Henry Newman, a nineteenth-century English cardinal and theologian.

What led our Lord to weep over the dead, who could at a word restore him, nay, had it in purpose so to do? He wept from very sympathy with the grief of others. "When Jesus saw Mary weeping, and the Jews also weeping which came with her, He groaned in the spirit, and was troubled." It is the very nature of compassion or sympathy, as the word implies, to "rejoice with those who rejoice, and weep with those who weep." We know it is so with men; and God tells us he also is compassionate. . . . Yet we do not well know what this means, for how can God rejoice or grieve? By the very perfection of his nature Almighty God cannot show sympathy, at least to the comprehension of beings of such limited minds as ours. . . . Words and works of sympathy he does display to us; but it is the very sight of sympathy in another that affects and comforts the sufferer more even than the fruits of it.

Now we cannot see God's sympathy; and the Son of God, though feeling for us as great compassion as his Father, did not show it to us while he remained in his Father's bosom. But when he took flesh and appeared on earth, he showed us the Godhead in a new manifestation. He invested himself with a new set of attributes, those of our flesh, taking into him a human soul and body, in order that thoughts, feelings, affections might be his, which could respond to ours and certify to us his tender mercy. When, then, our savior weeps from sympathy at Mary's tears, let us not say it is the love of a man overcome by natural feeling. It is the love of God, the compassion of the Almighty and Eternal, condescending to show it as we are capable of receiving it, in the form of human nature.

Jesus wept, therefore, not merely from the deep thoughts of his understanding, but from spontaneous tenderness. . . . [The] tears [of the people around him] touched him at once, as their miseries had brought him down from heaven. His ear was open to them, and the sound of weeping went at once to his heart.

Between Discussions

Mary, Martha, and Lazarus appear in John's Gospel (11:1–12:8). The sisters, without Lazarus, appear in Luke's Gospel also (Luke 10:38–42). The women display some of the same characteristics in both accounts: Martha does more of the talking and handles practical arrangements; Mary is more expressive of her devotion—sitting silently at Jesus' feet while he teaches (Luke 10:39), prostrating herself (11:32), and anointing him with scented oil (12:3). We are told so little about Lazarus that it is impossible to get a sense of his personality.

Their village, Bethany, was on the eastern slope of the Mount of Olives, a couple of miles east of Jerusalem. The site is now an Arab neighborhood called el-Azariyeh—from "Lazarus." The Franciscan fathers maintain a church there. Visitors are shown a tomb traditionally considered that of Lazarus, which does seem to date from the first century.

From all we can tell, Martha, Mary, and Lazarus were ordinary people. Their names were quite common—all have appeared in first-century burial inscriptions in the Jerusalem area. In one instance, all three names were discovered in a single tomb. The family was not wealthy, for they did not have servants serving the meals (12:2; Luke 10:40). But they were not impoverished either: many people came from Jerusalem to mourn for Lazarus (11:19, 45), the family could seat a dozen or so people in their dining area (12:1–2—apparently Jesus' disciples were with him), and they had expensive perfume in the house (12:3). One scholar writes that they were "reasonably well-off."

The three also seem to have been ordinary inasmuch as tranquillity did not always reign in their household (Luke 10:40). On occasion they tried to drag their honored guest into their disagreements—which suggests that Jesus was not an unapproachable figure around whom everyone felt they must constantly display their best behavior. Martha and Mary seem to have related to him as one of the family, even while they treated him with great respect.

Martha, Mary, and Lazarus are examples of Jesus' stay-at-home disciples. Their mention shows, as Ben Witherington writes, that Jesus "had not only traveling disciples, but also followers who remained in one place and offered Jesus and the disciples hospitality when they were in the area. This . . . means that Jesus did not require all his true followers to leave home and family in order to meet the demands of discipleship."

The family were friends not just of Jesus but of his disciples as well. Notice that Jesus speaks to his disciples of "*our* friend Lazarus" (11:11). While Luke 10 mentions only Jesus visiting Martha and Mary, John shows Jesus visiting the family with his traveling companions. Possibly the family hosted Jesus and his disciples whenever they were in the Jerusalem area for festivals.

The picture of Jesus and his companions sharing a meal in the home of nontraveling disciples (12:1–2) would have struck a familiar note for the Christians for whom John was writing. In their day, the Church met in homes, for there were no church buildings. Community members with homes large enough to accommodate visitors hosted meetings and provided accommodations for traveling missionaries.

We glimpse this pattern of life in Acts of the Apostles, which shows that the larger homes of believers were centers of life for the first Christian community in Jerusalem (Acts 1:13, 15; 12:12; 16:14–15, 40; 20:7–8). Larger households were apparently centers for care for the needy, for the community seems to have provided for poorer members by sharing meals with them, not simply by distributing funds (Acts 6:1 refers literally to daily table service). These meals did not take place in soup kitchens, but in people's houses. People coming and going for social and business reasons in such homes would be exposed to the gospel as believers told of the impact Jesus had had on their lives.

The brief scene of Jesus with Martha and Mary in Luke's Gospel has been well remembered in Christian tradition as a reminder of the priority of listening to Jesus over serving him. Perhaps we should also treasure the picture of Martha, Mary, and Lazarus entertaining Jesus and his companions (12:1–8) as an image of how nontraveling disciples of Jesus may use their homes in service to him.

PERFUME AND PALMS

Questions to Begin

15 minutes
Use a question or two to get warmed up for the reading.

1   What is the most delightful odor you have ever smelled?

2   How do you make use of hand creams, lotions, scented oils?

3   When have you realized that you failed to sufficiently appreciate someone's good qualities or their efforts on your behalf?

Opening the Bible

5 minutes
Read the passage aloud. Let individuals take turns reading
paragraphs.

The Reading: John 11:45–53; 12:1–33

The Authorities Reach a Decision

45 Many of the Jews therefore, who had come with Mary and had seen what Jesus did, believed in him. 46 But some of them went to the Pharisees and told them what he had done. 47 So the chief priests and the Pharisees called a meeting of the council, and said, "What are we to do? This man is performing many signs. 48 If we let him go on like this, everyone will believe in him, and the Romans will come and destroy both our holy place and our nation." 49 But one of them, Caiaphas, who was high priest that year, said to them, "You know nothing at all! 50 You do not understand that it is better for you to have one man die for the people than to have the whole nation destroyed." 51 He did not say this on his own, but being high priest that year he prophesied that Jesus was about to die for the nation, 52 and not for the nation only, but to gather into one the dispersed children of God. 53 So from that day on they planned to put him to death. . . .

The King Arrives, Prepared to Die

12:1 Six days before the Passover Jesus came to Bethany, the home of Lazarus, whom he had raised from the dead. 2 There they gave a dinner for him. Martha served, and Lazarus was one of those at the table with him. 3 Mary took a pound of costly perfume made of pure nard, anointed Jesus' feet, and wiped them with her hair. The house was filled with the fragrance of the perfume. 4 But Judas Iscariot, one of his disciples (the one who was about to betray him), said, 5 "Why was this perfume not sold for three hundred denarii and the money given to the poor?" 6 (He said this not because he cared about the poor, but because he was a thief; he kept the common purse and used to steal what was put into it.) 7 Jesus said, "Leave her alone. She bought it so that she might keep it for the day of my burial. 8 You always have the poor with you, but you do not always have me.". . .

12 The next day the great crowd that had come to the festival heard that Jesus was coming to Jerusalem. 13 So they took branches of palm trees and went out to meet him, shouting,

"Hosanna!
Blessed is the one who comes in the name of the Lord—
    the King of Israel!"
14 Jesus found a young donkey and sat on it; as it is written:
    15 "Do not be afraid, daughter of Zion.
    Look, your king is coming,
        sitting on a donkey's colt!"
16 His disciples did not understand these things at first; but when Jesus was glorified, then they remembered that these things had been written of him and had been done to him. 17 So the crowd that had been with him when he called Lazarus out of the tomb and raised him from the dead continued to testify. 18 It was also because they heard that he had performed this sign that the crowd went to meet him. 19 The Pharisees then said to one another, "You see, you can do nothing. Look, the world has gone after him!"

The Work Comes to an End

20 Now among those who went up to worship at the festival were some Greeks. 21 They came to Philip, who was from Bethsaida in Galilee, and said to him, "Sir, we wish to see Jesus." 22 Philip went and told Andrew; then Andrew and Philip went and told Jesus. 23 Jesus answered them, "The hour has come for the Son of Man to be glorified. 24 Very truly, I tell you, unless a grain of wheat falls into the earth and dies, it remains just a single grain; but if it dies, it bears much fruit. 25 Those who love their life lose it, and those who hate their life in this world will keep it for eternal life. 26 Whoever serves me must follow me, and where I am, there will my servant be also. Whoever serves me, the Father will honor.
    27 "Now my soul is troubled. And what should I say— 'Father, save me from this hour'? No, it is for this reason that I have come to this hour. 28 Father, glorify your name." Then a voice came from heaven, "I have glorified it, and I will glorify it again." 29 The crowd standing there heard it and said that it was thunder. Others said, "An angel has spoken to him." 30 Jesus answered, "This voice has come for your sake, not for mine. 31 Now is the judgment of this world; now the ruler of this world will be driven out. 32 And I, when I am lifted up from the earth, will draw all people to myself." 33 He said this to indicate the kind of death he was to die.

10 minutes
Choose questions according to your interest and time.

1 A denarius was a day's pay for a manual laborer. How much would Mary's nard (12:3, 5) be worth by today's standards?

2 In his response to Judas (12:7–8), does Jesus excuse his followers from caring for people who are in need? What does he mean?

3 Why does Jesus take the arrival of Greek-speaking inquirers (12:21–23) as the signal that the hour of his death and resurrection has come? (Consider these statements about the purpose of his death: 11:51–52; 12:32.)

4 In the Greek, it is possible to read Jesus' words in 12:27 as his prayer: "Father, save me from this hour!" This was how St. John Chrysostom interpreted these words (see page 35). How would this reading change the picture of Jesus in this verse?

A good leader helps the members of the group discover biblical truths for themselves.

Neil F. McBride, *How to Lead Small Groups*

A Guide to the Reading

*If participants have not read this section already, read it aloud.
Otherwise go on to "Questions for Application."*

The Jewish leaders on the temple council may have known that Jesus had no intention of establishing a political kingdom. But they felt threatened by his claims about himself and by the crowds that gathered around him (6:14–15), as dictatorships feel nervous about crowds today. The Romans expected the temple council to maintain public order and nip any buds of rebellion. If the council allowed a messianic movement to start rolling, the Romans would dismiss the members and find more reliable collaborators. Council members say literally that the Romans will *"remove from us"* the people and the temple (11:48). They are less concerned about protecting the people from Roman repression than about maintaining their own cozy, profitable relationship with the Romans.

Caiaphas's advice (11:50) may be translated "better . . . to have one man die *in place of* the people." Jesus will suffer in our place in order to preserve our lives and gather us to the Father (11:52). The high priest's unwitting statement of this truth illustrates God's sovereign ability to co-opt human opposition. If we resist him, God can use us to attain his goals nonetheless.

Jesus reclines at a festive meal beside the man he has raised from death (12:1–2)—a striking image of the purpose Jesus' death will serve. Through his death, Jesus will raise up all his friends, so that we may enjoy an intimate—and unending—celebration with him.

Reclining diners rested on their left arm, their heads facing toward the center of the dining area and their legs stretched out behind them. Thus Mary did not have to crawl under table and chairs to perform her striking act of honor and affection (12:3). Biblical scholar Rudolph Schnackenburg writes: "Mary has recognized the dignity and greatness of Jesus." Still, she may not have grasped the full significance of her action (12:7). Perhaps her love for Jesus has outdistanced her understanding of him. By receiving Mary's anointing as a preparation for burial (12:7), Jesus shows that *he* foresees and accepts the death that he is about to undergo. He will proceed to Jerusalem prepared to complete his work through suffering and death.

The next day, as he approaches the city, people greet him with palm branches, as though he were a Jewish military hero (see 1 Maccabees 13:51). They acclaim him as "the one who comes"—a messianic title taken from Psalm 118:26, to which they add the nationalistic title "the King of Israel" (12:13). Jesus, however, rejects their expectations. To express his own view of his kingship, he mounts a donkey and rides it into the city (12:14)—a prophetic gesture that identifies him as the humble king who will "command peace to the nations" (Zechariah 9:9–10). Biblical scholar George R. Beasley-Murray writes, "Nothing further from a nationalistic view of the messiah could be imagined." Jesus has come to draw to himself not only Jewish men and women but all men and women (11:52; 12:32). John underlines the non-nationalistic quality of Jesus' kingship by citing a prophecy that looks forward to a king under whom people from all over the earth will seek refuge in God's presence (12:15; compare Zephaniah 3:16–17). Jesus comes to bring peace from sea to sea—and his followers will have the obligation to pursue his vision of peace in the world.

Jesus has reached the end of his public mission; the time has come for him to be "glorified" (12:23). He will now be revealed as the Son who loves the Father totally. Jesus declares that anyone who follows him must likewise be dedicated to God's will, even if that means losing one's life (12:24–26). I am reminded of the statement of an acquaintance of mine, a priest who teaches in the Congo: Jesus calls us to devote ourselves to "God's project" in the world, no matter what it costs us.

The Father's words to Jesus (12:28) proclaim that God's life-giving love for men and women has been revealed throughout Jesus' public life and will now be revealed in the Father's gift to the world of his Son on the cross. Jesus will now be "lifted up" (12:32). The term can refer either to hanging up a criminal in execution or to raising up someone who is bowed down. Here it has both meanings. Jesus will be hung up on a cross, and this will be his exaltation to God's presence. Jesus' crucifixion will seem to be a humiliating failure, but it will actually be his enthronement as king of all—and Satan's dethronement (12:31).

Questions for Application

40 minutes
Choose questions according to your interest and time.

1 Sometimes people think that if only they could see a miracle, they would believe in God. What does the response of the religious authorities to Jesus' miracles (11:45–53) suggest about this line of thinking?

2 Mary was lavish with the Lord. What are ways of being lavish with the Lord today? When have you been lavish with the Lord?

3 Judas implies there is a conflict between serving needy people and honoring Jesus (12:5). What do you think?

4 The crowd that welcomes Jesus to Jerusalem honors him on the basis of mistaken expectations about what he is going to do. In what way does maturing in faith mean changing one's expectations about how God will act? How have you experienced this kind of change?

5 Jesus refused a nationalistic mission on behalf of the chosen people. What kind of nationalism—reflected in immigration policies, trade policies, and military policies, etc.—is appropriate or inappropriate for his followers to promote in their modern nations? How seriously should we consider the social justice implications of policies our government might undertake for nationalistic reasons?

6 Jesus entered Jerusalem as a king of universal peace. What obligations do his followers have to pursue his vision of peace in the world? Concretely, what does this mean for you?

7 Think of other figures besides Jesus, either historical or contemporary, whose suffering advanced their cause. What did their weakness do for their cause that stronger tactics might not have achieved? What can you learn from their experiences?

8 What does it mean to be prepared for death? Are you prepared?

Approach to Prayer

15 minutes
Use this approach—or create your own!

◆ Ask someone to slowly read aloud John 12:24–26.

Let each person silently consider this question: If I am a seed designed to die with Christ in order to bear fruit with him, what situation in my life is the ground where God wishes to plant me?

After a time of reflection, pray the Our Father together slowly as a way of expressing to God your willingness to die to your own desires and plans in order to play your part in the coming of his kingdom—and as a way of expressing your need for his help (the nourishment of "daily bread" from heaven!).

Looking ahead: Next week's "Approach to Prayer" requires preparation.

A Living Tradition

Jesus' Dread of Death

This section is a supplement for individual reading.

St. John Chrysostom, a prominent fourth-century bishop who lived in what is now southern Turkey, offered his parishioners this reflection on John 12:27–28 as part of a series of early morning talks on John's Gospel.

"Now my soul is troubled. And what shall I say? 'Father, save me from this hour!'" Surely this isn't the prayer of a person who is trying to persuade others to go toward death (12:25)? Indeed, it *is* the prayer of one who is urging precisely that. Jesus prays this way so that people cannot say, "He takes a calm, philosophical approach to death because he is immune to human pain. He gives us advice without being in any danger himself." By his prayer, he shows that although his death causes him anguish, nevertheless, on account of its usefulness for us, he does not refuse it. This is why he says, "Now my soul is troubled" . . . so troubled that he even demands release, if escape is possible. This is the weakness of human nature. . . .

"But even though I'm begging for release," he says, "wondering 'what should I say?' is not really where I'm at, for 'it is for this reason that I have come to this hour' (12:27)."

It is as though Jesus said to us, "Even if we are disturbed, even if we are troubled, let us not flee death, since I myself am troubled now, but I do not ask to escape, for I must bear what is coming toward me. I do not say, 'Release me from this hour.' But what do I pray? 'Father, glorify your name.' Even though this anguish forced me to say what I did, on the contrary I say, 'Glorify your name!' that is, 'Lead me at last to the cross.'"

This very clearly shows Jesus' humanity—his human nature not wishing to die but clinging to the present life. It is evidence that he was not immune to human pain. . . . Christ had a body free of sin but not free from natural stresses, since that would not have been a real human body.

Through these words Jesus taught us something else: if ever we are in a state of anguish and timidity, we should not turn away from the things that are set before us.

Between Discussions

In our next session we will begin to read John's account of the Last Supper. If we are familiar with the accounts of the Last Supper in the other three Gospels, in which Jesus' last meal is depicted as a Passover celebration (Matthew 26:17–30; Mark 14:12–26; Luke 22:7–39), we may simply assume that it is a Passover meal in John's account also. But John does not say that it is, nor does he narrate any details that identify it as a Passover meal. Furthermore, he goes on to relate that Jesus died on the evening when Passover began, that is, the evening when the Passover meal was eaten (18:28; 19:42). Thus in John's account, Jesus ate his final meal with his disciples on the night *before* Passover, and the meal seems not to be a Passover meal. What are we to make of this discrepancy between John and the other Gospel accounts?

Saints and scholars have tried to harmonize the two accounts, but none of the attempts is entirely convincing. One scholar, for example, has suggested that Jesus followed a slightly different calendar from that of most Jews—a calendar on which Passover began a day earlier. Thus Jesus both ate the Passover meal (on the special calendar) and died on the day when Passover was beginning (on the more general calendar). But there are problems with this explanation, and it has not persuaded most scholars. Thus the discrepancy remains unexplained.

It is relevant that other discrepancies regarding timing may be found among the Gospel accounts. In the first three Gospels, for instance, Jesus' public ministry seems to last less than a year; in John, more than two years. These differences may reflect the processes by which the Gospels came into existence. For some years after Jesus' life on earth, the good news about him was communicated mainly by word of mouth. Over three or more decades, different oral traditions developed. These traditions came to the Gospel writers in episodes that may no longer have carried clear time markers. The evangelists put them together in the best sequences they could. In general, they arranged the reports about Jesus' activities and teachings in ways that best bring out their meaning. The bishops at Vatican Council II, in the 1960s, touched on this process when they wrote, "The sacred authors wrote the four Gospels, selecting some things from the many which had been handed on by word of mouth or in writing, reducing some of them to a synthesis, explaining some things in view of the situation of their churches, and preserving the form of proclamation but always in such fashion that they told us the honest truth about Jesus" (*Dogmatic Constitution on Divine Revelation,* section 19).

Given these processes of oral tradition and Gospel writing, it may not be possible to determine conclusively which version of the timing of the Last Supper and Jesus' death is historically correct. This is an unresolved question, but perhaps it will be resolved in the future on the basis of new historical information or new insights.

Should this make us uncomfortable? We have to accept the Gospels as they are, not as we might wish them to be. They are basically historical. As Vatican II declared, "Holy Mother Church has firmly and with absolute constancy held, and continues to hold, that the four Gospels . . . whose historical character the Church unhesitatingly asserts, faithfully hand on what Jesus Christ, while living among men, really did and taught for their eternal salvation" (*Divine Revelation,* section 19). But they are not modern historical writing. The writers of the Gospels conveyed history in a form that helps us know not only what occurred but what it meant; not only what Jesus did but who he is, and what his words and actions mean for us today.

As for the history of the final events of Jesus' life, it is clear that Jesus ate a very important meal with his disciples the night before he died, and that the meal and his death occurred in conjunction with the Passover. Whatever the precise timing, the connection between Jesus' death and the Passover celebration is a key for interpreting the meaning of his death—a key that Jesus himself seems to have intended to give us. Passover celebrated the event through which God brought his people out of slavery in order to form a lasting relationship—a covenant—with them. The connection of Jesus' death with Passover signifies that his death also accomplishes a "bringing out from slavery" and a "covenant making"— a bringing out from sin and death, a covenant of eternal life.

LOVE TO THE END

Questions to Begin

15 minutes
Use a question or two to get warmed up for the reading.

1 When have you found it especially difficult to let someone perform some service (great or small) for you?

2 What was the most difficult service you ever performed for another person? How did the experience affect you? Would you do it again?

5 minutes
Read the passage aloud. Let individuals take turns reading
paragraphs.

The Reading: John 13

A Lesson in Loving

13:1 Now before the festival of the Passover, Jesus knew that his hour had come to depart from this world and go to the Father. Having loved his own who were in the world, he loved them to the end.

2 The devil had already put it into the heart of Judas son of Simon Iscariot to betray him. And during supper 3 Jesus, knowing that the Father had given all things into his hands, and that he had come from God and was going to God, 4 got up from the table, took off his outer robe, and tied a towel around himself. 5 Then he poured water into a basin and began to wash the disciples' feet and to wipe them with the towel that was tied around him. 6 He came to Simon Peter, who said to him, "Lord, are you going to wash my feet?" 7 Jesus answered, "You do not know now what I am doing, but later you will understand." 8 Peter said to him, "You will never wash my feet." Jesus answered, "Unless I wash you, you have no share with me." 9 Simon Peter said to him, "Lord, not my feet only but also my hands and my head!" 10 Jesus said to him, "One who has bathed does not need to wash, except for the feet, but is entirely clean. And you are clean, though not all of you." 11 For he knew who was to betray him. . . .

12 After he had washed their feet, had put on his robe, and had returned to the table, he said to them, "Do you know what I have done to you? 13 You call me Teacher and Lord—and you are right, for that is what I am. 14 So if I, your Lord and Teacher, have washed your feet, you also ought to wash one another's feet. 15 For I have set you an example, that you also should do as I have done to you. 16 Very truly, I tell you, servants are not greater than their master, nor are messengers greater than the one who sent them. 17 If you know these things, you are blessed if you do them. 18 I am not speaking of all of you; I know whom I have chosen. But it is to fulfill the scripture, 'The one who ate my bread has lifted his heel against me.' 19 I tell you this now, before it occurs, so that when it does occur, you may believe that I am he. 20 Very truly, I tell you, whoever receives one whom I send receives me; and whoever receives me receives him who sent me."

Jesus Speaks to His Betrayer

21 After saying this Jesus was troubled in spirit, and declared, "Very truly, I tell you, one of you will betray me." 22 The disciples looked at one another, uncertain of whom he was speaking. 23 One of his disciples—the one whom Jesus loved—was reclining next to him; 24 Simon Peter therefore motioned to him to ask Jesus of whom he was speaking. 25 So while reclining next to Jesus, he asked him, "Lord, who is it?" 26 Jesus answered, "It is the one to whom I give this piece of bread when I have dipped it in the dish." So when he had dipped the piece of bread, he gave it to Judas son of Simon Iscariot. 27 After he received the piece of bread, Satan entered into him. Jesus said to him, "Do quickly what you are going to do." 28 Now no one at the table knew why he said this to him. 29 Some thought that, because Judas had the common purse, Jesus was telling him, "Buy what we need for the festival"; or, that he should give something to the poor. 30 So, after receiving the piece of bread, he immediately went out. And it was night.

Jesus Gives Peter a Troubling Prediction

31 When he had gone out, Jesus said, "Now the Son of Man has been glorified, and God has been glorified in him. 32 If God has been glorified in him, God will also glorify him in himself and will glorify him at once. 33 Little children, I am with you only a little longer. You will look for me; and as I said to the Jews so now I say to you, 'Where I am going, you cannot come.' 34 I give you a new commandment, that you love one another. Just as I have loved you, you also should love one another. 35 By this everyone will know that you are my disciples, if you have love for one another."

36 Simon Peter said to him, "Lord, where are you going?" Jesus answered, "Where I am going, you cannot follow me now; but you will follow afterward." 37 Peter said to him, "Lord, why can I not follow you now? I will lay down my life for you." 38 Jesus answered, "Will you lay down your life for me? Very truly, I tell you, before the cock crows, you will have denied me three times."

10 minutes
Choose questions according to your interest and time.

1 What double meaning might there be in John's statement (13:1) that Jesus "loved them to the end"?

2 How would you interpret Peter's protest against Jesus' washing his feet (13:6, 8)?

3 For whom is Jesus troubled in verse 21? Compare Jesus' emotional reaction here with his reaction in 11:33 (the same Greek word is used in both verses, translated "troubled" in 13:21 and "deeply moved" in 11:33). How are these two situations similar? What might this tell us about Jesus?

4 What double meaning might there be in the end of verse 30?

5 What word or two would you use to characterize how Jesus relates to his disciples in this reading? to describe how his disciples relate to him?

A Guide to the Reading

*If participants have not read this section already, read it aloud.
Otherwise go on to "Questions for Application."*

Up to this point in John's Gospel, Jesus has made it clear to his disciples that he expects them to believe in him and accept him as their source of nourishment and life (6:51–58; 7:37–39), but he has given little instruction about how they should live as his followers. Only now, literally on the eve of his death, does he explain the requirements of discipleship. The proximity of his teaching to his death is significant. Jesus calls us to a love and unity of which we are incapable; only his death—and the gift of the Spirit that his death brings—enables us to follow his teaching.

Jesus gets to the heart of his instruction with a simple gesture (13:1–11). John puts it in context (13:2–3)—a context we might expand by reading the account in light of the beginning of the gospel (1:1–3, 14): In the beginning was the Word, and the Word was with God, and the Word was God. All things came into being through him. The Word became a human being . . . and then, one night, in the middle of dinner, he got up from the table and washed his disciples' dirty feet. What an awesome demonstration of love—a love unimpeded by pride or self-concern.

Jesus' washing of his disciples' feet is more than they can understand at that moment (13:7), for it symbolizes something that has not yet happened: his death. John hints at the link between Jesus' foot washing and his dying when he says that Jesus *takes off* his robe (13:4), using (in the Greek) the same word Jesus has used for *laying down* his life (10:11, 15, 17, 18). There is another link: only slaves washed other people's feet, and only slaves and certain low-class criminals were crucified. Just as the water Jesus now pours over the disciples' feet washes away the dust of the road, his death the following day will cleanse them of their sins.

It is instructive to consider the men whose feet Jesus bathes. Most remarkably there is Judas. The Greek of verse 2 can be taken to mean that Satan has made up his mind to have Judas betray Jesus. If this is John's meaning, Judas himself may not yet have resolved to betray Jesus as he allows him to bathe and dry his feet. Jesus' offering of a piece of food to Judas (13:26)—an act of esteem by which a host singles out a guest whom he wishes to honor—is then an expression of friendship that brings Judas to the moment of decision. Jesus calls his wavering friend to quickly make up his mind what he is going to do (13:27). Judas's acceptance of the morsel without forsaking his plan to betray Jesus means that he has chosen Satan over God. Acting as a kind of representative of the world that rejects Jesus' revelation of God, Judas brings judgment on himself (see 3:16–21).

Peter is no traitor, but neither is he the loyal hero he considers himself to be. He declares his love (13:6–9) but will soon deny that he knows Jesus (18:15–18, 25–27). The other disciples seem peculiarly unperceptive (13:22, 29).

These are the disciples on whom Jesus lavishes his demonstration of humble service. Jesus loves them in their ignorance, failure, and betrayal.

This is the love that Jesus calls us to imitate (13:14–15, 34–35). It is a love that is not only humble enough to wash feet, but sincere enough in its humility to wash the feet of those who do not understand us, even those who are disloyal to us in our time of need, *even* those who do us harm. Peter is representative of us all as he struggles against this utterly self-giving love (13:8).

In verse 19 Jesus literally says, "so that . . . you may believe that *I am*." This *I am* is a form by which God refers to himself in the Old Testament (Isaiah 41:4; 48:12). Jesus is thus making a claim to divinity: in him, God is revealed. "Part of this revelation," writes Francis J. Moloney, "is his choice of a group of ignorant, failing disciples, one of whom will betray him. . . . Jesus' never-failing love for *such* disciples, a love that reached out even to the archetype of the evil disciple, reveals a unique God." On any Sunday morning we may look around the church and marvel that God is the kind of person who chooses such imperfect people as ourselves and our fellow worshipers to be close to him, to carry out his mission in the world, to be his friends.

Questions for Application

40 minutes
Choose questions according to your interest and time.

1   Jesus calls his disciples to follow his "example" and love as he has loved (13:15, 34). Judging from the way Jesus relates to Peter, Judas, and his other disciples in this reading, what does Jesus mean by love? What are the similarities and differences between love in this sense and love as most people think of it today?

2   What might be a modern equivalent of washing feet? What would most people think of a leader—in government, business, or some other field—who performed such a service for those he or she was leading?

3   What are the strengths in Peter's relationship with Jesus? What does Peter lack? What are the strengths and weaknesses in your own relationship with Jesus? What do Jesus' responses to Peter suggest about Jesus' relationship with you?

4 How can a person let Jesus wash his or her feet today?

5 Is it really possible or psychologically healthy to love someone who has betrayed you or has done you serious harm? When have you witnessed or experienced love like that of Jesus—love given even in the face of misunderstanding or betrayal? When have you tried to love in this way?

6 In what situation could you take Jesus' washing of his disciples' feet as a model for your behavior? What would you do differently in that situation?

When the leader rushes from question to question, keeping a tight rein on discussion, the group tends to become rigid and mechanical. . . . If you wait, others will share their thoughts.

Gladys Hunt, *Gladys Hunt's "How-To" Handbook for Inductive Bible Study Leaders*

Approach to Prayer

15 minutes
Use this approach—or create your own!

◆ Pray together this prayer,
adapted from a prayer by
St. Anselm.

Jesus, how easy it is to ask your
    blessing on my friends.
Now, with your Spirit's help, I
    bring before you what I desire
for my enemies and for those who
    have injured me.

But first, merciful Lord, I ask that
    you yourself inspire those
    desires.
Whatever you lead me to ask for
    my enemies,
give it to them and give the same
    back to me.
And so, dear Jesus, I ask you
to lead my enemies into your light,
    your truth, your love—
and me along with them.
Let us be reconciled to you and to
    one another, according to
    your will.

O merciful Judge,
forgive me all my debts, as I now
    forgive all those who are
    indebted to me.
I cannot do this perfectly yet.
But know, Lord, that I wish to
and that I will do all I can to
    forgive from the heart.

A New Commandment

This section is a supplement for individual reading.

Jesus described his command to love as something new: "I give you a new commandment, that you love one another. Just as I have loved you, you also should love one another" (13:34). Here are some reflections on these words from St. Thérèse of Lisieux, a nineteenth-century French Carmelite nun.

At the time when God commanded the chosen people to love their neighbor as themselves, Jesus had not yet come upon the earth. Knowing how much we each love our own selves, this was the greatest love that God could ask us to show others. But when Jesus gives his apostles a new commandment—his own commandment—he says to love our neighbor not as we love ourselves but as *he* loves them and will love them till the end of time. . . .

Lord, I know that you don't command the impossible. You know my weakness and imperfection better than I do. My Jesus, you know well that I will never be able to love my Sisters as you love them unless you yourself love them in me.

It is because you wanted to give this grace that you gave us a new commandment. How I love it, since it gives me assurance that your will is to love in me all those people you command me to love! . . .

I know that whenever I am charitable, it is Jesus alone who is working in me. The more closely united I am with him, the more I love all my Sisters. Whenever the devil tries to confront me with a Sister's faults—especially a Sister I don't especially like—I try to grow in this love by quickly recalling her virtues and good intentions. I tell myself that while I've seen her fall once, she may well have won many victories which she humbly keeps to herself. Also, even something that appears to me a fault may well be an act of virtue because of her intention. I have no trouble persuading myself that this may be the case, for I've had this experience myself.

Between Discussions

Death often comes in ways that do not allow for proper good-byes. The death that rushes up suddenly on the express-way and the death that ends a long period of mental decline leave no opportunity for last words. Those who have some warning of their departure, however, have the chance to bring some closure to their relationships with family and friends. They can collect their thoughts and consider what they most want to leave with those who will continue on in this world. Their words of farewell are likely to be remembered.

Jesus was one of those who knew that death was approaching, and all four Gospels show him gathering his disciples shortly before the end of his life to give them final instructions and reassurance. In John's account, Jesus speaks to them at length in the intimate atmosphere of a final meal. As we have seen, the meal begins with two incidents that must have astonished the disciples: Jesus gets down on the floor and washes their feet; then he announces that one of them will betray him. Before they can regain their balance after these disturbing developments, Jesus leads them into a conversation about his plans in which they struggle to keep pace with what he is trying to communicate (13:31–14:24). After a while, the conversation becomes a mono-logue. Jesus speaks at length as the disciples listen in silence, perhaps comforted by his voice and presence even if they do not entirely grasp his meaning (14:25–16:33). Finally, Jesus sums up his words—and his entire life—in a solemn prayer (chapter 17).

Because this is Jesus' farewell address, his words are especially weighty. More than some of his earlier statements, his words seem aimed more directly at us who read the Gospel. In the Bible, a number of persons deliver farewell speeches—Jacob, Moses, David, Paul (Genesis 49; Deuteronomy 31–34; 1 Kings 2:1–9; Acts 20:17–38). In each case the speaker not only reflects on his own life but looks ahead into the lives of those who will come after him. The dying one senses the challenges that will arise and gives advice about how to meet them. Because of this concern for the future, the farewell addresses seem to later readers as though they were spoken directly to them. In John's account, Jesus speaks to his disciples not mainly about their present situation that night in Jerusalem but about the years ahead, after his death and resurrection. Significantly, at one point in his prayer, Jesus explicitly mentions those of us who will be reading the Gospel in later years: he asks his Father to care for "those who will believe in me through their word" (17:20). That's us, who have come to faith through the preaching of his disciples. Thus we have every reason to pay particularly close attention to Jesus' words in chapters 13 to 17.

Yet many readers would admit that these chapters are not easy going. The reader who likes to have a clear idea of where the speaker is headed and how his ideas fit together may feel frustrated. Jesus does not proceed in a linear fashion, but loops back to subjects he has already dealt with. Even more challenging is Jesus' use of luminously simple words and images—*way, vine, dwell*—to express the most profound realities about our relationship with God. Here, above all in John's Gospel, we will do well to take seriously the Latin maxim *festina lente*—"make haste slowly!" This section of John calls for quiet meditative reading and re-reading, a little at a time.

In this frame of mind, let us quietly enter the Last Supper room, take our places among the disciples, and listen as Jesus expresses the thoughts that are deepest in his heart on the night before his death. We are the ones who have believed through the words of his disciples. He is speaking to us.

No Need to Fear

Questions to Begin

15 minutes
Use a question or two to get warmed up for the reading.

1 Have you or someone in your family ever inherited anything? What was it? What effect did the inheritance have on you or the person who inherited it?

2 People are often deeply impressed by their last conversation with someone who is about to die. Have you had such a conversation? What impression did it make on you?

5 minutes
Read the passage aloud. Let individuals take turns reading paragraphs.

The Reading: John 14

What the Disciples Can Expect

14:1 "Do not let your hearts be troubled. Believe in God, believe also in me. 2 In my Father's house there are many dwelling places. If it were not so, would I have told you that I go to prepare a place for you? 3 And if I go and prepare a place for you, I will come again and will take you to myself, so that where I am, there you may be also. 4 And you know the way to the place where I am going."

5 Thomas said to him, "Lord, we do not know where you are going. How can we know the way?"

6 Jesus said to him, "I am the way, and the truth, and the life. No one comes to the Father except through me. 7 If you know me, you will know my Father also. From now on you do know him and have seen him."

8 Philip said to him, "Lord, show us the Father, and we will be satisfied."

9 Jesus said to him, "Have I been with you all this time, Philip, and you still do not know me? Whoever has seen me has seen the Father. How can you say, 'Show us the Father'? 10 Do you not believe that I am in the Father and the Father is in me? The words that I say to you I do not speak on my own; but the Father who dwells in me does his works. 11 Believe me that I am in the Father and the Father is in me; but if you do not, then believe me because of the works themselves. 12 Very truly, I tell you, the one who believes in me will also do the works that I do and, in fact, will do greater works than these, because I am going to the Father. 13 I will do whatever you ask in my name, so that the Father may be glorified in the Son. 14 If in my name you ask me for anything, I will do it.

How Jesus Will Be Absent Yet Present

15 "If you love me, you will keep my commandments. 16 And I will ask the Father, and he will give you another Advocate, to be with you forever. 17 This is the Spirit of truth, whom the world cannot receive, because it neither sees him nor knows him. You know him, because he abides with you, and he will be in you.

18 "I will not leave you orphaned; I am coming to you. 19 In a little while the world will no longer see me, but you will see me; because I live, you also will live. 20 On that day you will know that I am in my Father, and you in me, and I in you. 21 They who have my commandments and keep them are those who love me; and those who love me will be loved by my Father, and I will love them and reveal myself to them."

Where God Will Make His Home

22 Judas (not Iscariot) said to him, "Lord, how is it that you will reveal yourself to us, and not to the world?"

23 Jesus answered him, "Those who love me will keep my word, and my Father will love them, and we will come to them and make our home with them. 24 Whoever does not love me does not keep my words; and the word that you hear is not mine, but is from the Father who sent me.

25 "I have said these things to you while I am still with you. 26 But the Advocate, the Holy Spirit, whom the Father will send in my name, will teach you everything, and remind you of all that I have said to you. 27 Peace I leave with you; my peace I give to you. I do not give to you as the world gives. Do not let your hearts be troubled, and do not let them be afraid. 28 You heard me say to you, 'I am going away, and I am coming to you.' If you loved me, you would rejoice that I am going to the Father, because the Father is greater than I. 29 And now I have told you this before it occurs, so that when it does occur, you may believe. 30 I will no longer talk much with you, for the ruler of this world is coming. He has no power over me; 31 but I do as the Father has commanded me, so that the world may know that I love the Father. Rise, let us be on our way."

10 minutes
Choose questions according to your interest and time.

1 In verses 1 and 27 Jesus uses the word for "troubled" that earlier describes his own reactions (12:27; 13:21). How, then, would you explain his counsel in verses 1 and 27?

2 What does it mean to pray in the name of Jesus (14:14)?

3 Notice that Jesus speaks of the Spirit as "*another* Advocate" (14:16). What does this tell us about the Spirit—and about Jesus?

4 How well do Jesus' disciples understand him? How big a task will the Spirit have (14:26)?

5 After Jesus' departure, who will come and be with the disciples? Identify all the relevant statements in the reading. What can be learned by putting these statements together?

A Guide to the Reading

If participants have not read this section already, read it aloud. Otherwise go on to "Questions for Application."

Jesus has upset his disciples by announcing that one of them will betray him, that he is leaving them, and that one of them will reject him (13:21, 33, 38). Now (14:1) he tells them why, nevertheless, they can be at peace. He assures them that he is returning to heaven in order to prepare a place for them (14:2–3). Ben Witherington remarks that just as Jesus has acted as God's agent on earth, now he will act as our agent in heaven.

Jesus' friends need not worry about getting to the place that Jesus will prepare for them because he will also prepare the road that leads there. In fact, he will *be* the road—the living and true way to the Father (14:6). By coming into the world, Jesus has perfectly revealed God to men and women (14:7). By leaving the world via the cross, Jesus will reconcile men and women to God. By his twofold movement, Jesus becomes the bridge between God and humanity. Jesus is God's way into the world to humankind and humankind's way into heaven to God.

Jesus can be this bridge because he is both fully human (1:14) and fully God (1:1–2; 14:10–11). The disciples are still far from grasping this mystery, and we may well sympathize with them (14:8). But Jesus seems mildly exasperated with their incomprehension (14:9). Nevertheless he assures them that after his departure, he will work through them ("the one who believes in me will also do the works that *I do*"—14:12) to such a degree that they will accomplish more than he has so far accomplished!

All this indicates that after his departure Jesus will somehow continue his relationship with his followers. From verses 15 to 27 he elaborates on how this will be. In basic terms, Jesus tells his disciples that as he goes away, another person like himself will come and take his place. He calls this person the "Advocate" (14:16). The Greek word here is so hard to translate that some versions simply bring it over unchanged from the Greek: "Paraclete." This is Jesus' special term, used only in John's Gospel, for the Holy Spirit (14:26). Biblical scholar Raymond E. Brown, S.S., comments, "John presents the Paraclete as the Holy Spirit in a special role, namely, as the personal presence of Jesus in the Christian while Jesus is with the Father. . . . Since the Paraclete can come only when Jesus departs [16:7], the Paraclete is the presence of Jesus when Jesus is absent. . . . It is no accident that the first passage containing Jesus' promise of the Paraclete (14:16–17) is followed immediately by the verse which says, 'I am coming back to you' [14:18]."

After Jesus rises from the dead, he will make a few brief appearances to his disciples. But by the Spirit, he will remain with his disciples throughout all time (14:16–18). Jesus promises to reveal himself to each of us by the Spirit in a way that corresponds to his post-Resurrection appearances to his first disciples (14:21). Since Jesus and the Father are inseparable, when Jesus, by the Spirit, comes to abide in his followers, the Father will come too (14:23). Thus Jesus departs to make a dwelling place for us with the Father and returns in the Spirit to make a dwelling place for the Father in us.

Jesus' description of the Paraclete, or Advocate, in verse 17 might be translated "the Spirit who conveys truth." The Spirit will take up Jesus' mission of revealing the life-giving God to us. The Spirit will not teach anything radically new but will make Jesus' revelation of the Father alive and present to us. Thus Jesus says that the Spirit will *remind* the disciples of what Jesus has said to them. The Spirit will not bring a new teaching; he will help the disciples grasp the wealth of the teaching that Jesus has already given them. Just as Jesus has revealed the Father, the Spirit will reveal Jesus who reveals the Father.

Throughout his ministry Jesus has emphasized the crucial importance of belief in himself, and he continues to do so here (14:1, 11, 12). Now in addition to believing in him, he also calls us to love him (14:15, 21, 23, 24). The context in which Jesus speaks of his own "love" for his Father (14:31—the only time in John's Gospel that Jesus explicitly speaks of his own love for the Father) makes it clear that this love involves obedience and trust (see also 15:10). Jesus will glorify the Father through his love by obeying and trusting the Father and by carrying out the Father's saving project even to death. By these acts Jesus will demonstrate how lovable, trustworthy, and deserving of devotion God really is.

Questions for Application

40 minutes
Choose questions according to your interest and time.

1 Jesus tells us not to be troubled in verse 1. Does he mean "don't experience fear or sorrow"?

2 What reasons for his reassurance does Jesus give in this reading? In what situation do you most need to remember his message?

3 When have you experienced peace as a result of putting faith in Jesus? How should this affect how you live today?

4 In verse 12 Jesus speaks of his followers doing greater "works" than he has done. Earlier he used this word to refer to miraculous healing (7:21) and also to something broader (4:34; see also 17:4). Look at these passages. What does Jesus mean by his statement in verse 12? What implications do his words have for your life?

5 How can Christians open themselves to the action of the Holy Spirit? How do you open yourself to the Spirit's action?

6 Sometimes Christians feel sorry that they did not see and hear Jesus during his earthly life. What about you? How does this reading respond to that attitude?

7 Which of Jesus' statements in this reading most seems like his personal word to you? Why? In what area of your life does it have most meaning? How should you respond to it?

Don't get discouraged because there is so much to cover. You have a lifetime to read and reread the Bible.

Rena Duff, *Sharing God's Word Today*

Approach to Prayer

15 minutes
Use this approach—or create your own!

◆ Pray a Hail Mary. Let someone in the group read the following meditation by biblical scholar William S. Kurz, S.J.

Everything temporal is also temporary. . . . Peace based on any earthly arrangement . . . must of its nature pass away. Success, riches, health, power, popularity . . . are all imper-manent. So is any peace based on them. . . . Since worldly kinds of peace perish in death, "He who loves his life loses it . . ." (John 12:25). . . . To surrender to God all one's deepest desires brings a psychological experience of "losing one's life." . . . But Christ's peace is unattainable without such a loss. . . . Only surrender to God of one's life, of all one's hopes, desires, and fears, in submission to God's perfect will for oneself, will open the way for Christ's lasting peace to enter.

Pause for silent reflection on John 14:27: "My peace I give to you." End by praying together the Our Father.

Saints in the Making
Peace at a Low Point

This section is a supplement for individual reading.

Bob Mitchell, a member of St. Olaf's Church in Poulsbo, Washington, in his seventies, developed an infection in his artificial knee that also threatened his mechanical heart valve. Despite a two-week hospital stay, around-the-clock anti-biotics, and devoted care by his wife, Toni, the infection persisted. Doctors decided that the best course of action was to remove Bob's artificial knee for several weeks until the infection subsided. The alternative was for Bob to go home and continue on antibiotics there. Hoping to avoid surgery, Bob and Toni, who is a nurse, decided to return home.

At home, despite the infusion of antibiotics, Bob continued to run a fever. "I was getting discouraged and worried," he recounts. "One night I couldn't sleep, so I got up and read the Scripture reading for that day in *God's Word Today* magazine. The reading was John 14:1–14. The first verse jumped out at me: 'Do not let your hearts be troubled. You have faith in God; have faith also in me.' After reading the verse several times, I turned to the commentary. One paragraph was so beautiful that I felt renewed reading it:

Speaking to his disciples Jesus uses the same word that has repeatedly described his own state of soul: "troubled" (11:33; 12:27; 13:21). His comfort, then, does not mean, "If you have faith in me you won't ever feel disturbed"; after all, he himself knows what it means to be deeply disturbed. His meaning is closer to: "When you are troubled, remain united with me. I go through the troubles of this life into eternal life. If you remain in me, you will find a peace greater than your troubles."

"Every day I would go back to that Scripture verse and commentary, and I continued to get fresh strength from the words."

In the weeks that followed, Bob's temperature returned to normal, and all signs of the infection disappeared. "I don't know whether it was all the prayers from our friends at church, prayers from our family, or our own prayers," Bob says. "I only know that I am so thankful to God for leading me to the Scripture that gave me such peace at my lowest point."

Between Discussions

After our target reading in Week 4, we skip over a considerable portion of John's Gospel. Our reading in Week 5 will open with Jesus, already condemned to death, carrying his cross to Golgotha. Here is a brief summary of the intervening section.

Despite the apparent conclusion of Jesus' farewell address in 14:31, he goes on to speak to his disciples for two more chapters (15–16). Many scholars think that the author or editor of the Gospel inserted this material after chapter 14 but for some reason did not remove the conclusion that had ended that chapter.

In chapters 15 and 16 Jesus continues to reassure his disciples, but this reassurance is based on the continuation of their relationship with him, not on a promise that their lives will be trouble free. Jesus illustrates the depth of their bond with him by the analogy of a grapevine (15:1–10). He is the vine, they are the branches. Someone has pointed out that Jesus does not say that he is the trunk and the disciples the branches; he is the whole vine, of which the branches are a part. Jesus, in effect, makes us part of himself. Paul makes the same basic point by saying that we are members of Christ's body (1 Corinthians 12:27). Men and women who share so deeply in Jesus' life will express that life as naturally as a grapevine bears grapes (15:4–5). Since the essence of Jesus' divine life is love, love is the fruit that we bear from our union with him. It is a love that is shared, first of all, among those who are together rooted in Jesus' life (15:9–17).

But the love that Jesus has shown in the world has not found favor with everyone. Indeed, rejection of his revelation of God's love has become so intense that his enemies are about to have him put to death. Jesus' love will continue to encounter resistance as it manifests itself through his disciples. As the world has hated me, Jesus warns them, it will hate you, and for the same reasons (15:18–16:4). Jesus' coming into the world has caused a division between those who open themselves to God's revelation and those who close themselves off. When the Spirit arrives, he will continue to provoke the same sort of division among people, but it will be the disciples rather than Jesus who will be in the forefront of the conflict (16:4–15). This is a frightening prospect for the disciples, but Jesus steadies them with two reassurances. In his absence, his relationship with them will actually be stronger than ever (16:16–24). And his death and resurrection will deliver a radical blow to the powers of evil that resist God (16:25–33).

Jesus draws the long meal to a close with a prayer in which he offers himself and his followers to the Father and asks that God keep them in his truth and love while they are in the world (chapter 17). His words resemble the eucharistic prayer of the Mass.

After this, the protracted stillness of the dining room gives way to a rapid flow of events. Jesus walks with his disciples down the hill from Jerusalem and across the moonlit stones of the dry Kidron Valley to an olive grove on the hill opposite the city (18:1). Having already portrayed Jesus' distress and prayer in the face of his oncoming death (12:27–28), the Gospel of John passes over any prayer in the garden. Almost immediately, Judas arrives with a band of Roman soldiers and police sent by the temple authorities (18:3). The fact that they seize Jesus but let his followers go (18:4–11) indicates the authorities' awareness that Jesus has not been trying to organize a revolt against the Roman occupation.

The temple authorities interrogate Jesus but do not conduct a full-scale trial (18:12–14, 19–24)—they have already decided to have him put to death (11:45–53). Jesus declares that he has spoken openly to everyone; anyone wishing to know his teaching can ask his followers (18:20–21). At that very moment Peter, the most prominent of his followers, is denying that he even knows Jesus (18:15–18, 25–27)!

The temple authorities soon hand Jesus over to the Roman governor, who has the authority to impose capital punishment. The governor, Pontius Pilate, becomes convinced that Jesus poses no threat to the Roman regime. But to please the religious authorities, he condemns him to death. In the process, Jesus finally speaks openly of his kingship, declaring that it is a prophetic kingship, a kingship that exercises authority not by military force but by speaking the truth (18:37).

THE KING IS LIFTED UP

Questions to Begin

15 minutes
Use a question or two to get warmed up for the reading.

1 Have you ever been in a situation in which someone risked their life for someone else? How were you involved? What impact did the event have on you?

2 Besides your parents, has anyone else played a fatherly or motherly role in your life? Describe the relationship. What effect has this person had on you?

5 minutes
Read the passage aloud. Let individuals take turns reading
paragraphs.

The Reading: John 19:16–42

Jesus Is Crucified

16 So they took Jesus; 17 and carrying the cross by himself, he went out to what is called The Place of the Skull, which in Hebrew is called Golgotha. 18 There they crucified him, and with him two others, one on either side, with Jesus between them. 19 Pilate also had an inscription written and put on the cross. It read, "Jesus of Nazareth, the King of the Jews." 20 Many of the Jews read this inscription, because the place where Jesus was crucified was near the city; and it was written in Hebrew, in Latin, and in Greek. 21 Then the chief priests of the Jews said to Pilate, "Do not write, 'The King of the Jews,' but, 'This man said, I am King of the Jews.'" 22 Pilate answered, "What I have written I have written." 23 When the soldiers had crucified Jesus, they took his clothes and divided them into four parts, one for each soldier. They also took his tunic; now the tunic was seamless, woven in one piece from the top. 24 So they said to one another, "Let us not tear it, but cast lots for it to see who will get it." This was to fulfill what the scripture says,
"They divided my clothes among themselves,
    and for my clothing they cast lots."
25 And that is what the soldiers did.

The Work Is Completed

Meanwhile, standing near the cross of Jesus were his mother, and his mother's sister, Mary the wife of Clopas, and Mary Magdalene. 26 When Jesus saw his mother and the disciple whom he loved standing beside her, he said to his mother, "Woman, here is your son." 27 Then he said to the disciple, "Here is your mother." And from that hour the disciple took her into his own home.
    28 After this, when Jesus knew that all was now finished, he said (in order to fulfill the scripture), "I am thirsty." 29 A jar full of sour wine was standing there. So they put a sponge full of the wine on a branch of hyssop and held it to his mouth. 30 When Jesus had received the wine, he said, "It is finished." Then he bowed his head and gave up his spirit.

31 Since it was the day of Preparation, the Jews did not want the bodies left on the cross during the sabbath, especially because that sabbath was a day of great solemnity. So they asked Pilate to have the legs of the crucified men broken and the bodies removed. 32 Then the soldiers came and broke the legs of the first and of the other who had been crucified with him. 33 But when they came to Jesus and saw that he was already dead, they did not break his legs. 34 Instead, one of the soldiers pierced his side with a spear, and at once blood and water came out. 35 (He who saw this has testified so that you also may believe. His testimony is true, and he knows that he tells the truth.) 36 These things occurred so that the scripture might be fulfilled, "None of his bones shall be broken." 37 And again another passage of scripture says, "They will look on the one whom they have pierced."

A Royal Burial

38 After these things, Joseph of Arimathea, who was a disciple of Jesus, though a secret one because of his fear of the Jews, asked Pilate to let him take away the body of Jesus. Pilate gave him permission; so he came and removed his body. 39 Nicodemus, who had at first come to Jesus by night, also came, bringing a mixture of myrrh and aloes, weighing about a hundred pounds. 40 They took the body of Jesus and wrapped it with the spices in linen cloths, according to the burial custom of the Jews. 41 Now there was a garden in the place where he was crucified, and in the garden there was a new tomb in which no one had ever been laid. 42 And so, because it was the Jewish day of Preparation, and the tomb was nearby, they laid Jesus there.

10 minutes
Choose questions according to your interest and time.

1 Why might Pilate have refused to change the inscription on the cross (19:22)? (There is no one right answer.)

2 Jesus' declaration of thirst (19:28) may remind the reader of an earlier incident in which Jesus is thirsty: 4:7–15. How might the conversation between Jesus and the Samaritan woman shed light on the meaning of Jesus' death?

3 What do Jesus' last words mean (19:30)?

4 Jesus' legs not being broken (19:31–36) is an allusion to the lamb killed for the Passover celebration (Exodus 12:46). This, in turn, is a reminder of John the Baptist's words about Jesus (1:29–34). How might John the Baptist's words help to explain the significance of Jesus' death?

A Guide to the Reading

*If participants have not read this section already, read it aloud.
Otherwise go on to "Questions for Application."*

It was cruel and humiliating—and common practice—to make the victim of crucifixion carry the horizontal section of the cross to which he was about to be nailed (19:17). The image of Jesus doing so is a reminder of an earlier biblical incident, in which the boy Isaac carried the wood on which he himself was to be sacrificed (Genesis 22:6). Abraham's willingness to sacrifice his son Isaac gives an insight into what is happening as Jesus staggers toward Golgotha: here too a grief-stricken Father is relinquishing his only Son to a sacrificial death.

Pilate insists on writing that Jesus is the king of the Jews (19:19–22). What irony! The placard, declaring Jesus' kingship in the three leading languages of the day, makes a fool of Jesus before the whole world—yet it proclaims the truth. Jesus *is* the king who will draw people of every language and land to himself. His enemies—here Pilate, earlier Caiaphas (11:49–52)—unwittingly acknowledge his kingship and his saving role—a phenomenon that signals his ultimate conquest of the powers of evil which at this moment engulf him (12:31–32).

John focuses our attention on Jesus' clothing (19:23). The seamlessness of the garment testifies to his adherence to the Mosaic law. A garment would be woven in one piece to guard against the possibility of breaking the rule against combining two kinds of cloth (Deuteronomy 22:11). Tearing a garment had once symbolized dividing a kingdom (1 Kings 11:29–32). St. Cyprian, a third-century African bishop, saw Jesus' untorn robe as a sign of the unity of the Church. We cannot possess the garment of Christ, that is, his kingdom, Cyprian said, unless we remain united to his whole Church in faith and love.

Jesus entrusts his mother to the care of his closest disciple. At the same time, his mother becomes a gift to the disciple—and to all disciples (19:25–27). This man and woman, brought together at the cross, symbolize the entire new community—the Church— that Jesus will create by his death.

Jesus' cry of thirst (a terrible echo of 4:7) and the soldier's response (19:28–29) allude to a psalm in which a person endures desolation and scorn but hopes for vindication by God

(Psalm 69:19–21). At the moment of death, Jesus "hands over," or "delivers," the spirit (19:30). This is not a euphemism for death, but John's way of showing that Jesus' death opens the way for the Spirit to come. Francis Moloney writes, "In bringing to perfection the task the Father had given to him Jesus hands over, entrusts, the Spirit to his new family gathered at the foot of the cross."

Breaking the legs of crucified men quickly brought death by asphyxiation, since they could no longer push themselves up to breathe. That Jesus' legs are left intact (19:33, 36) alludes to another righteous sufferer who trusted in God (Psalm 34:20) and to the Passover lamb (Exodus 12:46). The branch of hyssop (19:29) is a reminder of the sprinkling of the Passover lamb's blood on the doorpost of the Israelites' houses at the Exodus (Exodus 12:22). Like the Passover lamb, whose blood spared men and women from judgment, Jesus has died so that we might escape the judgment that falls on sin.

A soldier stabs at Jesus' apparently lifeless body, testing for a reaction (19:34). Scourging (19:1) may have caused blood and watery fluid to accumulate in Jesus' traumatized chest cavity (19:34–35). Jesus spoke earlier of water flowing from his chest— a reference to the gift of the Spirit (7:38). This suggests that the spurt of water from his corpse symbolizes the Spirit that will flow from him after he rises. He had also spoken of his own blood, in his teaching about himself as the bread of life (6:53–56). The water and blood, then, symbolize the ways in which Jesus will continue to make his life accessible to us—in the gift of the Spirit in baptism and in the gift of his body and blood in the Eucharist.

Joseph's asking Pilate for Jesus' body for burial was an act of courage (19:38). Up to this point Joseph and Nicodemus have been afraid to be publicly identified as followers of Jesus (3:1–2; 19:38). Jesus' death now spurs them to demonstrate their love— an initial sign of the effect his death will have on his followers. Nicodemus brings an enormous quantity of expensive spices (19:39). In death, Jesus is recognized as king (compare 2 Chronicles 16:14). Indeed, only now that he has given his life on the cross can the nature of his kingship begin to be understood.

Questions for Application

40 minutes
Choose questions according to your interest and time.

1 What message would Jesus' crucifixion have communicated to the residents of Jerusalem who witnessed it? How might this message have been different from the view that John conveys?

2 The relatives and friends of Jesus could not do anything for him as he died. When have you had the experience of being with, yet unable to help, someone who was in pain or difficulty? Is such presence useless?

3 How have you experienced God's love in the midst of suffering? How has this affected your view of life and of God?

4 Have you ever seen a bond develop between people who go through suffering together (for example, sharing in the care for a sick relative or friend)? What have you learned from this?

5 When has love for someone inspired you to undertake something dangerous or difficult for them? Looking back on it, do you wish you had done something different? How did this experience affect you?

6 Perhaps for private reflection: What effect has God's forgiveness had on you? How should your experience of his forgiveness affect how you relate to other people?

The more careful and thorough your observations, the more meaningful will be your interpretations, and the richer will be your applications.

Oletta Wald, *The Joy of Discovery*

Approach to Prayer

15 minutes
Use this approach—or create your own!

◆ Pray together the prayer by
Caryll Houselander on the
following page. Pause for silent
reflection or any spontaneous
prayers that anyone wishes to
express. Close with the Hail
Mary.

Prayer to Jesus Crucified

This section is a supplement for individual reading.

A prayer by Caryll Houselander, a mid-twentieth-century English psychologist and author.

Lord,
wholly surrendered
to the will of Your Father
and wholly identified with us,
Lord nailed to the cross
by Your own choosing,
teach us to obey,
to accept,
to bow to the will of God.

Give us wisdom
and the strength
to pledge ourselves,
to bind ourselves irrevocably
to the law of Your love.
Let us so bind ourselves
that we will not only
adhere to You
in times of consolation,
in times of sweetness and devotion
and when life goes smoothly,
but yet more securely
in the bleak and bitter
seasons of the soul—
in the hard iron of the winters
of the spirit.

Between Discussions

Christian spirituality has taken many forms. Some forms may seem accessible, almost familiar to us, even across many centuries. Others closer in time may seem puzzling and remote. While the life of Francis of Assisi and his first followers in the thirteenth century may seem fresh and appealing, aspects of the religious sensibility of French laypeople in the nineteenth century may seem strange to us. But we can learn something from all the expressions of spiritual life in the Church by focusing on the personal devotion to Jesus that lies at the center of them all . . .

In July 1887, in France, Henri Pranzini was condemned to death for murder. A fourteen-year-old girl, Thérèse Martin, followed his story in the newspapers and decided to pray for him. Here is how she recounted her experience some years later.

One Sunday as I was looking at a picture of Our Lord on the cross, I was struck by the sight of the blood falling from one of his divine hands. I felt a great pang of sorrow at the thought that this blood was flowing onto the ground without anyone bothering to collect it, and I resolved to remain in spirit at the foot of the cross to gather up this heavenly dew and give it to others. . . . Jesus' cry on the cross resounded constantly in my heart: "I thirst!" (John 19:28). These words enkindled in me a new and burning love. . . . I longed to give my Beloved a drink, and I felt consumed by the thirst for souls. . . .

I heard people talk about a notorious criminal named Pranzini who had just been sentenced to death for horrible crimes. All signs indicated that he was going to die without repenting. I wanted at all costs to save him from going to hell, so I made use of every spiritual means I could. Knowing that I couldn't do anything of myself, I offered God the infinite merits of Our Lord and the treasures of the Church. . . . Deep down in my heart, I felt certain that my desire would be satisfied. Still, to encourage myself to keep praying for sinners, I prayed very simply: "My God, I'm very certain that you will forgive this wretched Pranzini. I have so much confidence in the infinite mercy of Jesus that I will believe this, even if Pranzini doesn't go to confession or give any sign of repentance. But still, for my own consolation, please give me just one 'sign.'". . .

Papa never used to let us read the papers, but I didn't consider myself disobedient when I read the sections that concerned Pranzini. The day after his execution, I rushed to the newspaper *La Croix*, and what did I see? . . . I was so moved that my eyes filled with tears and I had to rush away. . . . Pranzini had not gone to confession. He had climbed up the scaffold and was about to put his head on the block when, moved by a sudden inspiration, he turned around, seized the crucifix that the priest was holding out, and kissed Jesus' sacred wounds three times! . . . I had obtained the "sign" I had asked for—a sign modeled after the very graces through which Jesus had drawn me to pray for sinners. Hadn't the thirst for souls entered my heart as I contemplated the blood flowing from one of Jesus' wounds? . . . What a wonderful answer! . . .

After this special grace, my desire to save souls grew day by day. I seemed to hear Jesus saying, "Give me to drink," as he did to the Samaritan woman (John 4:7). It was a real exchange of love: to souls, I offered Jesus' blood; to Jesus, I offered the same souls, now cleansed by the dew of Calvary. The more I worked to quench his thirst, the greater became my own. . . . In a short time, God had led me out of my narrow world. . . . I had taken the first step, but the road ahead was long.

Outwardly, Thérèse's road was very narrow indeed—the world of a Carmelite convent. She entered the convent at the age of fifteen and spent the rest of her short life there, dying at the age of twenty-four. This restricted world, however, proved to be the ideal environment for her growth in faith and love of God. Her prayer for people throughout the world grew so deep that, despite the confinement of her convent life, she is considered to be a patron of missionaries. In fact, as St. Thérèse of Lisieux, she is honored with the title "doctor," that is, "teacher" of the Church.

WHY ARE YOU WEEPING?

Questions to Begin

15 minutes
Use a question or two to get warmed up for the reading.

1 When has something happened to you that was almost too good to be true?

2 Are people inclined to take a man's testimony more seriously than a woman's, or vice versa? What is your experience of this?

5 minutes
Read the passage aloud. Let individuals take turns reading
paragraphs.

The Reading: John 20

A Burial Undone

[1] Early on the first day of the week, while it was still dark, Mary
Magdalene came to the tomb and saw that the stone had been
removed from the tomb. [2] So she ran and went to Simon Peter and the
other disciple, the one whom Jesus loved, and said to them, "They
have taken the Lord out of the tomb, and we do not know where they
have laid him." [3] Then Peter and the other disciple set out and went
toward the tomb. [4] The two were running together, but the other
disciple outran Peter and reached the tomb first. [5] He bent down to
look in and saw the linen wrappings lying there, but he did not go in.
[6] Then Simon Peter came, following him, and went into the tomb. He
saw the linen wrappings lying there, [7] and the cloth that had been on
Jesus' head, not lying with the linen wrappings but rolled up in a
place by itself. [8] Then the other disciple, who reached the tomb first,
also went in, and he saw and believed; [9] for as yet they did not understand the scripture, that he must rise from the dead. [10] Then the
disciples returned to their homes.

The Risen One Reveals Himself

[11] But Mary stood weeping outside the tomb. As she wept, she bent
over to look into the tomb; [12] and she saw two angels in white, sitting
where the body of Jesus had been lying, one at the head and the other
at the feet. [13] They said to her, "Woman, why are you weeping?" She
said to them, "They have taken away my Lord, and I do not know
where they have laid him." [14] When she had said this, she turned
around and saw Jesus standing there, but she did not know that it
was Jesus. [15] Jesus said to her, "Woman, why are you weeping? Whom
are you looking for?" Supposing him to be the gardener, she said to
him, "Sir, if you have carried him away, tell me where you have laid
him, and I will take him away." [16] Jesus said to her, "Mary!" She
turned and said to him in Hebrew, "Rabbouni!" (which means
Teacher). [17] Jesus said to her, "Do not hold on to me, because I have
not yet ascended to the Father. But go to my brothers and say to
them, 'I am ascending to my Father and your Father, to my God and
your God.'" [18] Mary Magdalene went and announced to the disciples,

"I have seen the Lord"; and she told them that he had said these things to her.

When it was evening on that day, the first day of the week, and the doors of the house where the disciples had met were locked for fear of the Jews, Jesus came and stood among them and said, "Peace be with you." 20 After he said this, he showed them his hands and his side. Then the disciples rejoiced when they saw the Lord. 21 Jesus said to them again, "Peace be with you. As the Father has sent me, so I send you." 22 When he had said this, he breathed on them and said to them, "Receive the Holy Spirit. 23 If you forgive the sins of any, they are forgiven them; if you retain the sins of any, they are retained."

Seeing, Not Seeing, and Believing

24 But Thomas (who was called the Twin), one of the twelve, was not with them when Jesus came. 25 So the other disciples told him, "We have seen the Lord." But he said to them, "Unless I see the mark of the nails in his hands, and put my finger in the mark of the nails and my hand in his side, I will not believe."

26 A week later his disciples were again in the house, and Thomas was with them. Although the doors were shut, Jesus came and stood among them and said, "Peace be with you." 27 Then he said to Thomas, "Put your finger here and see my hands. Reach out your hand and put it in my side. Do not doubt but believe." 28 Thomas answered him, "My Lord and my God!" 29 Jesus said to him, "Have you believed because you have seen me? Blessed are those who have not seen and yet have come to believe."

30 Now Jesus did many other signs in the presence of his disciples, which are not written in this book. 31 But these are written so that you may come to believe that Jesus is the Messiah, the Son of God, and that through believing you may have life in his name.

10 minutes
Choose questions according to your interest and time.

1 Chapter 20 is composed of two sections (20:1–18 and 20:19–29). What is the climax of each section?

2 Compare Jesus' burial clothes (20:5–7) to those of Lazarus (11:44). What are the differences? What might be the significance of these differences? (More than one explanation is possible.)

3 Compare Mary's tears for Jesus outside his tomb with Jesus' tears for Lazarus (11:35). How are they similar? How are they different?

4 Throughout the Gospel Jesus has spoken of God as *his* Father but not as the *disciples'* Father. Against this background, what is the significance of verse 17? (Take a look also at 1:12.)

5 How much impact does Mary's report (20:18) have on the disciples?

6 Was Thomas's skepticism (20:25) well-founded? Why or why not?

A Guide to the Reading

If participants have not read this section already, read it aloud. Otherwise go on to "Questions for Application."

John has shown that Jesus' words often contained unexpected meanings (recall, "Lazarus has fallen asleep"—11:11). Perhaps Jesus couched whatever predictions he gave his disciples about his resurrection in such puzzling terms that his meaning escaped them. Misunderstanding would be especially likely if they thought of resurrection as an event that occurs only at the end of time (Martha's belief—11:24). In any case, the disciples seem totally unprepared for what they find at Jesus' tomb.

When Mary Magdalene discovers the tomb opened she immediately suspects grave robbery—a common crime. But inside the tomb Peter and "the other disciple" find evidence that does not support this conclusion (20:6–8). Grave robbers would be interested in the costly linens and spices (19:39–40). Why would they carry away a worthless corpse and leave the valuable wrappings—even taking the trouble to arrange them neatly?

Apparently John sees something significant in the disposition of the wrappings, but scholars cannot agree on what it is. Some argue that the cloths retained the shape of Jesus' head and body, indicating that he had exited from them in a miraculous manner. But if this were the case, why wouldn't Peter realize what had happened? Notice the contrast between Jesus' burial wrappings and those of Lazarus. Lazarus came forth from the tomb wearing the clothes of death (11:44), while Jesus has left every vestige of death behind. He has not returned to temporary, earthly life, like Lazarus, but has risen into eternal life with God.

Weeping outside the tomb, Mary Magdalene resembles Mary of Bethany at Lazarus's tomb (11:33): she loves Jesus deeply but does not understand that he is the resurrection. Jesus brought the dead Lazarus back into life by calling him by name. Now he summons Mary by name so that she may rise from the grave of her hopelessness into the joy of knowing him in his risen life (20:16). Raymond Brown suggests that we too will recognize Jesus' presence as we hear his word spoken in the Church.

Mary wants to cling to Jesus' physical presence. She does not understand that it is not yet time to cling to him. Jesus is in the process of ascending to the Father ("I'm on my way," he says—20:17). When his ascension is complete, he will give the Spirit, and through the Spirit she will be able to cling to him always.

Presumably Mary needs no command to tell the disciples that she has seen Jesus. But Jesus entrusts her with a message about the significance of his resurrection (20:17). For the first time in this Gospel, he speaks of God as the *disciples'* Father. Through Jesus' death and resurrection, his own relationship of intimate love with God is now shared with us who believe in him (see 1:12–13).

In the evening, Jesus appears to a group of his disciples. He greets them in an everyday manner, but with what extraordinary meaning! It is easy to say, "Peace," but here is someone who truly *delivers* peace—the one who has overcome death and has opened the way to eternal life with God. And it is not simply the sight of him risen that brings his followers peace; it is the gift of the Spirit (20:22). Jesus' appearance will soon end; his Spirit will remain.

While Jesus gives his Spirit to all his followers, he gives the leaders of his community a special authorization to make present the restored relationship with God that he has accomplished (20:23). The Church assures us that this reconciliation is always accessible to us through the sacrament of Reconciliation.

One disciple proves resistant to the news that Jesus has risen. Thomas rejects the apostolic testimony—the testimony on which all succeeding generations of Christians will rely (20:25). But when Jesus shows himself, Thomas utters the acknowledgment of Jesus toward which the entire Gospel has been moving: "My Lord and my God." *Finally* someone recognizes who Jesus is. As George Beasley-Murray points out, Thomas's statement is not merely a theological definition but a deeply personal expression of faith in who Jesus is for Thomas. "The personal pronoun is of vital importance: '*My* Lord and *my* God.'"

In response, it is as though Jesus turns from the roomful of disciples and looks out toward the readers of the Gospel in every age (20:29). Addressing himself to us, he declares, "Blessed are *you* who have not seen and yet have come to believe!"

Questions for Application

40 minutes
Choose questions according to your interest and time.

1 Which person in this reading do you identify with the most? Why?

2 What would Jesus' "Peace be with you" (20:19) have meant to his disciples at that moment? What do his words mean for you today?

3 What is the connection between forgiveness and peace for an individual? for a group? for a nation?

4 What signs of Jesus' resurrection are most important for your faith? In what way is faith in Jesus a gift? How can a person grow in faith?

5 Consider the ways in this chapter that "the disciple Jesus loved," Mary Magdalene, the group of the disciples, and Thomas come to believe that Jesus is risen. What similarities and differences do you see between their experiences and the ways that people come to faith in Jesus today?

6 What incident in the readings from John's Gospel in these six sessions has made the deepest impression on you? What makes it so important for you? How might it play a part in your life and your prayer?

Whoever thinks that he understands the divine Scriptures in such a way that his interpretation does not build the double love of God and of our neighbor does not understand it at all.

St. Augustine, *On Christian Teaching*

Approach to Prayer

15 minutes
Use this approach—or create your own!

♦ Pray together this prayer of John Henry Newman.

My God, the Paraclete, I acknowledge thee as the Giver of that great gift, by which alone we are saved: supernatural love. . . . By the fire which thou didst kindle within us, we pray, and meditate, and do penance. As well could our bodies live, if the sun were extinguished, as our souls if thou art away.

My most holy Lord and Sanctifier, whatever there is of good in me is thine. . . . Increase in me this grace of love, in spite of all my unworthiness. It is more precious than anything else in the world. I accept it in place of all the world can give me. O give it to me! It is my life.

Close with an Our Father.

This section is a supplement for individual reading.

Joan McTigue began working as a volunteer with parents of children with cerebral palsy because of her third child, a daughter who had cerebral palsy. Later, as assistant director of the adult program of the Rochester, New York, Cerebral Palsy Association, she worked for several years with adult victims of cerebral palsy.

At the same time, Joan was involved in the charismatic renewal. During a charismatic renewal conference in New Jersey, she read John 21:15–17 ("Feed my sheep") and had a mental image of her adult clients living in a Christian community. She felt a desire to do something for "God's lambs"—but what should she do? "When I shared this with my spiritual director, Father William Frankhauser," she says, "he invited me to work with him in forming a community for disabled people."

Father Frankhauser, a Jesuit priest, knew Jean Vanier, the founder of L'Arche, a community for developmentally disabled adults. Inspired by L'Arche, Father Frankhauser obtained the use of a downtown building and began to form a community of people with cerebral palsy and other disabilities. The handicapped people moved into the apartments, and with the help of aides they maintained as much independence as they could. Those who chose shared meals in a common dining room. Eventually twenty to twenty-five residents took part in the venture. Many people came during the day and evening for Mass and social activities.

Joan was heavily involved in the community. She did not live on the premises but came each day to lead activities. For a while she took care of lunches. Her husband, Jack, was also involved, as was one of their adult sons.

The community called itself IHS, which is both a traditional tag for the Jesuits (*IHS* are the first three letters of *Jesus* in Greek) and an abbreviation for Integrating the Handicapped into Society. The community flourished for several years before ill health caused Father Frankhauser to resign, and changing circumstances brought the community to an end.

For Joan McTigue, three words from John's Gospel—"feed my sheep"—had opened the door to years of rewarding service.

After Words

John has brought his Gospel to a close (20:31). But someone, perhaps a disciple of John, has added a final chapter—chapter 21. Clearly this disciple—some scholars call him "the editor"—is not the author of the rest of the Gospel, for he refers to the main author as another person (21:24). Thus the Gospel of John has two endings.

The second ending, however, is not out of keeping with the rest of the Gospel. The editor drew his material from the same tradition about Jesus that was the basis for the rest of the Gospel. He relates an incident in Galilee, where the disciples saw the first of Jesus' signs (2:1–12). His ending thus brings a sense of completion to the story by tying it back to its beginning.

Actually, it is a little surprising to find the disciples back in Galilee. After seeing the risen Jesus in Jerusalem, why have they gone home to their fishing (21:3) instead of going out into the world with the good news about Jesus? Quite likely, even after seeing Jesus and receiving the Spirit, they have not instantly grasped all the implications of Jesus' resurrection. Their return to Galilee may be a sign not of loss of faith but of the distance they still need to travel before they appreciate what Jesus' resurrection means for their lives. Most of us can identify with that.

As throughout the rest of John's Gospel, small details are significant. As a result of Jesus' direction, the disciples net an extraordinarily large catch ("It is notable that never in the Gospels do the disciples catch a fish without Jesus' help," Raymond Brown remarks), which Peter hauls ashore (21:5–11). The unbroken net (recall Jesus' undivided clothing—19:24) seems to symbolize the Christian community, which is not torn apart by the large number of diverse people it contains. The mere act of Peter's *drawing* the net is significant. Jesus predicted that through his death he would *draw* all men and women to himself (12:32). By using the same word here, the author suggests that Peter will play a part in this process.

Perceiving in Jesus' bread-and-fish breakfast an allusion to the multiplication of the loaves and fish (6:11) and to the Eucharist, early Christian artists sometimes adorned places where Christians assembled with a depiction of Jesus sharing bread and fish with seven disciples (21:2). No doubt these early Christians regarded this Gospel scene as a reminder of the heavenly banquet that believers will share with Jesus in the age to come.

Jesus uses the encounter with his disciples to rehabilitate Peter. The charcoal fire (21:9) reminds us of the one in the courtyard where Peter denied Jesus (18:18). Standing by this second fire, Jesus gives Peter an opportunity to replace his threefold denial with a threefold expression of loyalty (18:17, 25–27; 21:15–17). At the Last Supper, Jesus told Peter that Peter could not follow him. Peter had protested that he *would* follow Jesus even to death (13:36–38), but as Jesus predicted, Peter failed. Now Jesus does invite Peter to follow him even to death (21:18–19). Peter will be able to do it because Jesus has given his life for Peter and has breathed the Spirit into him.

Jesus not only asks Peter if Peter loves him; he tells Peter to care for his sheep. Thus Jesus not only renews his relationship with Peter; he gives him a commission. "Shepherd" is an ancient metaphor for ruler. Jesus, the shepherd of the flock of God's people, calls Peter to be his authorized representative. As Jesus has fulfilled his shepherding role by laying down his life, so he calls Peter to do also. Since the sheep continue to belong to Jesus ("*my* sheep"—21:16), Peter will tend them not for his own benefit but on behalf of their owner.

The commission is specific to Peter. The other disciples have faded into the background; Peter emerges from the group with a more important role (21:15). Apparently Jesus' ideal of "one flock, one shepherd" (10:16) will be realized through Peter, the one shepherd. The passage says nothing explicit about whether Peter's role will continue after his death. But it is significant that the editor of the Gospel thought it important to speak about Peter's authority some twenty or thirty years after his death. Apparently the editor thought Peter's role had continuing importance for Christians.

Washing Feet

Careful reading involves noticing what is on the page in front of you. It also involves noticing what is *not* there. As we read, our minds have an unconscious tendency to supply missing elements that we know should be present. This is why people often ask someone to check their work when they write a report, business letter, or class paper. The writer, who knows what he or she meant to write, might not notice if any words have been accidentally omitted. (It was only after repeated rereading that I realized I had at first omitted the *s* on *knows* in the preceding sentence.)

Many of us mentally fill in details when we read the Gospels. Without realizing it, we import information from the other Gospels into the one we are reading. This is often a useful process, but it may lead us to overlook significant differences between the evangelists' accounts. Investigating the evangelists' omissions may bring us to a deeper understanding of their message.

We meet an instance of this in John's account of the Last Supper. If you read all the way from chapter 13 to chapter 17, you will discover that John makes no mention of Jesus' praying the meal blessings and giving bread and wine to his disciples as his own body and blood (Matthew 26:26–29; Mark 14:22–25; Luke 22:15–20). Reading John's account, we may unconsciously add this action to our mental picture of the event. But the absence in John's Gospel of a narrative of the institution of the Eucharist is worth our attention.

Why does John not present an account of Jesus' institution of the Eucharist? It cannot be that he did not know about it. From chapter 6 it seems clear that, like other early Christians, John and his Christian community celebrated the Eucharist. Indeed, that chapter demonstrates a profound understanding of the Eucharist as a means by which Jesus remains united to his disciples after his departure.

Some scholars suspect that a portion of chapter 6 (6:51–58) started out as part of an account of Jesus' institution of the Eucharist at the Last Supper. Their theory is that the material was moved to chapter 6 so that these words of Jesus about the

Eucharist would be situated in a context that helps to explain what the Eucharist is all about (the rest of chapter 6). But there is no way to reach certainty about such a theory. And in any case, it leaves unanswered the question why John did not also recount the institution of the Eucharist at the Last Supper.

In any event, what is certain is that John has given us an account of the Last Supper that is similar to yet different from that of the other evangelists. In all accounts, it is an action Jesus performs a profoundly significant act in the course of the meal. In the other accounts, it is an action with bread and wine; in John, it is an action with water and a towel. Since the incident with the bread and wine is of central importance to the Christian faith, we may suspect that John's parallel—Jesus' washing of his disciples' feet—is also very important.

In the other Gospels, Jesus' sharing of himself in the bread and wine is his means of explaining the purpose of his death. As he gives the bread and the cup to his disciples, he not only tells them that these elements are now himself in the form of food ("this is my body . . . this is my blood"); but he also speaks about his body and blood in a way that shows what will be accomplished when he perishes on the cross. "This is my body, which is *given for you*" (Luke 22:19)—biblical language meaning that his life will be an offering, a sacrifice of reconciliation with God. "This is my blood *of the covenant, which is poured out for many for the forgiveness of sins*" (Matthew 26:28). That is to say, the flow of blood from his body will remove sins and establish an enduring relationship between God and human beings.

Likewise, by washing their feet Jesus offers his disciples an image that helps to interpret his death. Like washing feet, his voluntary death on the cross will be a humble service, willingly undertaken as an act of personal kindness for his friends. Just as the water of the washing loosens and removes the dirt from their feet, Jesus' death will dissolve their guilt and renew their minds and hearts. As the bathing of their feet makes them clean and refreshed for the meal of friendship with Jesus, so his dying for them will enable them to enjoy his friendship forever.

The parallel between the meal sharing and the foot washing of the Last Supper continues beyond the pages of the Gospels into the life of the Church, because in both cases Jesus told his disciples to imitate his action. Jesus instructed his disciples to continue to share his body and blood in the sacred meal of thanksgiving to God that he himself ate with them: "Do this in remembrance of me" (Luke 22:19). He also told his disciples to imitate his foot washing: "If I, your Lord and Teacher, have washed your feet, you also ought to wash one another's feet. For I have set you an example, that you also should do as I have done to you" (13:14–15).

Jesus' commission to his disciples regarding his action with bread and wine instituted the Eucharist, our central act of worship and communion with him. Here and there in the early Church, some Christian communities practiced a ceremonial foot washing also. But the Church did not finally accept foot washing as a fully sacramental action to be included in the Church's liturgical life (although a foot-washing ceremony is part of the liturgy of Holy Thursday, when we especially commemorate the Last Supper). Perhaps the reason that foot washing did not become recognized as a sacrament is that the forgiveness of sins and cleansing of mind and heart that it symbolizes are accomplished through two other sacraments—baptism and reconciliation. But Jesus' washing of his disciples' feet not only symbolized his cleansing of their persons; it demonstrated his willingness to take on the role of servant out of love for them. It is this aspect of his action that the Church has understood him to mean when he said, "You also ought to wash one another's feet" (13:14).

A similarity between the sacramental presence of Jesus in the Eucharist and his presence in the washing of feet is worth our consideration. The sacramental nature of the Eucharist brings a guarantee of Jesus' action and presence. When we celebrate the eucharistic liturgy, we can be sure that through Christ's words spoken by the priest and by the Spirit's action, bread and wine are changed into Jesus' body and blood (Catechism of the Catholic Church, sections 1353, 1375–76). Jesus becomes sacramentally present in a manner that surpasses every other mode of his presence with us (CCC, section 1373). Jesus does not promise us that he will act in a similarly *specific* way when we carry out his instructions about foot washing by assuming the role of servant in our ordinary lives. But he does promise us that when we adopt the role of servant and love those around us, he will be with us and will make himself known to others through us. After washing his disciples' feet, Jesus tells them, "I give you a new commandment, that you love one another. Just as I have loved you, you also should love one another. By this everyone will know that you are my disciples, if you have love for one another. . . . They who have my commandments and keep them are those who love me. . . . Those who love me will keep my word, and my Father will love them, and we will come to them and make our home with them" (13:34–35; 14:21, 23).

Thus there is a similarity between the confidence we can have that Jesus is present in the Eucharist and the confidence we can have in his presence when we humble ourselves to serve the needs of our fellow human beings. When the priest repeats the words of institution, by the power of the Holy Spirit bread and wine are truly changed into the body and blood of the Lord, and we renew our communion with him by receiving him in the sacrament. When we place ourselves in a position of service to other people, Jesus makes himself truly present, drawing us and those we serve toward himself and his Father. Catholics are accustomed to reflect on the high privilege that is given to the bishop and priest, for through their ministry the Lord makes himself sacramentally present to his people. John 13 spurs us to reflect on the high privilege that Jesus offers to all of us—the privilege of embodying his humble, sincere, and friendly love for all men and women.

Singing Praise

The Odes of Solomon are ancient prayers written in a dialect of Aramaic, the language that Jesus and his first followers spoke. No one knows for sure who wrote these forty-two psalmlike songs. But some scholars believe they were composed by Christians who were in touch with the tradition coming from "the disciple whom Jesus loved"—the disciple on whose testimony the Gospel of John is based. Quite possibly these prayers were written at the same time as John's Gospel. Certainly the writers of the odes wove into their prayers many of the distinctive thoughts and images that we find in John's Gospel. Here, in shortened and adapted form, are two of the odes.

In Ode 41, the "great day" of which the poet speaks is probably the day when the Word became flesh (1:14). John does not state that the Lord "shared with us his glory," but it sounds very much like the kind of thing that John *would* say. The poet's reference to "the Word who was with God from the beginning" expresses the same faith in Jesus that we find at the very beginning of John's Gospel (1:1–2).

Let all his little children praise the Lord,
    and let us receive his constant faithfulness.
He will acknowledge them in his presence as his sons and
      daughters,
    therefore let us sing in his love.
We live in the Lord by his goodness,
    and we receive life in his Messiah,
for he made a great day shine out for us,
    and to our amazement he shared with us his glory.
So let us all unite in the Lord
    and honor him in his goodness,
let our faces shine in his light
    and our hearts ponder his love night and day.
Let us exult with divine exultation!

His Word is with us in all our way—
    the savior who makes us live and does not reject us,
the man who humbled himself
    and was raised up in his holiness.

The Son of the Most High appeared
    in the perfection of his Father,
and light has dawned from the Word—
    who was with God from the beginning.
Truly the Messiah was known before the foundations of the
    world,
    that he might give eternal life to his people by his truth.
New praise for the Lord from those who love him!

The composer of Ode 39 seems to have been inspired both by the story of Jesus walking on the waters of the Sea of Galilee during a storm (6:16–21) and Jesus' claim to be the "way" to the Father (14:6). He imagines Jesus walking across the raging, flood-swollen rivers of earthly life, leaving immovable footsteps on the surface as a sure bridge to safety for those who follow him.

There are mighty rivers
    quicker than lightnings and swift,
but those who cross them in faith
    will not be disturbed,
and those who walk on them without fault
    will not be troubled,
because the Lord is the sign marked upon them
    and he is the Way of those who cross in his name.

Put on the Most High, then, and know him,
    so you may cross without danger
for he has made a bridge over the waters by his Word
    who walked across them on foot;
his footprints were established on the water and were not
    destroyed;
    no, they remain there like wood solidly built;
on both sides the waves rose up,
    but the footprints of our Lord the Messiah stand firm
and are not erased
    and are not changed.

The Way is appointed for those who cross after him
    and complete the walk of faith in him
and worship him. Alleluia!

Suggestions for Bible Discussion Groups

Like a camping trip, a Bible discussion group works best if you agree on where you're going and how you intend to get there. Many groups use their first meeting to consider such questions. Here is a checklist of issues, with bits of advice from people with experience in Bible discussions. (A planning discussion will go more smoothly if the leaders have thought through the following issues beforehand.)

Agree on your purpose. Are you getting together to gain wisdom and direction for your lives? to finally get acquainted with the Bible? to support one another in following Christ? to encourage those who are exploring—or reexploring—the Church? for other reasons?

Agree on attitudes. For example: "We're all beginners here." "We're here to help each other understand and respond to God's word." "We're not here to offer counseling or direction to each other." "We want to read Scripture prayerfully." What do *you* wish to emphasize? Make it explicit!

Agree on ground rules. Barbara J. Fleischer, in her useful book *Facilitating for Growth*, recommends that a group clearly state its approach to the following:

- ◆ Preparation. Do we agree to read the material and prepare the questions before each meeting?
- ◆ Attendance. What kind of priority will we give to our meetings?
- ◆ Self-revelation. Are we willing to help the others in the group gradually get to know us—our weaknesses as well as our strengths, our needs as well as our gifts?
- ◆ Listening. Will we commit ourselves to listen to each other?
- ◆ Confidentiality. Will we keep everything that is shared *with* the group *in* the group?
- ◆ Discretion. Will we refrain from sharing about the faults and sins of people outside the group?
- ◆ Encouragement and support. Will we give as well as receive?
- ◆ Participation. Will we give each person time and opportunity to make a contribution?

You could probably take a pen and draw a circle around *listening* and *confidentiality*. Those two points are especially important.

The following items could be added to Fleischer's list:

◆ Relationship with parish. Is our group part of the adult faith formation program? independent but operating with the express approval of the pastor? not a parish-based group at all?

◆ New members. In the course of the six meetings, will new members be allowed to join?

Agree on housekeeping.

◆ When will we meet?

◆ How often will we meet? Meeting weekly or every other week is best if you can manage it. William Riley remarks, "Meetings once a month are too distant from each other for the threads of the last session not to be lost" (*The Bible Study Group: An Owner's Manual*).

◆ How long will meetings run?

◆ Where will we meet?

◆ Is any setup needed? Christine Dodd writes that "the problem with meeting in a place like a church hall is that it can be very soul-destroying" given the cold, impersonal feel of many church facilities. If you have to meet in a church facility, Dodd recommends doing something to make the area homey (*Making Scripture Work*).

◆ Who will host the meetings? Leaders and hosts are not necessarily the same.

◆ Will we have refreshments? Who will provide them?

◆ What about childcare? Most experienced leaders of Bible discussion groups discourage bringing infants or other children to adult Bible discussions.

Agree on leadership. You need someone to facilitate—to keep the discussion on track, to see that everyone has a chance to speak, to help the group stay on schedule. Rena Duff, editor of the newsletter *Sharing God's Word Today,* recommends having two or three people take turns leading the discussions.

It's okay if the leader is not an expert regarding the Bible. You have this booklet, and if questions come up that no one can answer, you can delegate a participant to do a little research between meetings. It's important for the leader to set an example of listening, to draw out the quieter members (and occasionally restrain the more vocal ones), to move the group on when it gets stuck, to remind the members of their agreements, and to summarize what the group is accomplishing.

Bible discussion is an opportunity to experience the fulfillment of Jesus' promise "Where two or three are gathered in my name, I am there among them" (Matthew 18:20). Put your discussion group in Jesus' hands. Pray for the guidance of the Spirit. And have a great time exploring God's word together!

Y ou can use this booklet just as well for individual study as for group discussion. While discussing the Bible with other people can be a rich experience, there are advantages to individual reading. For example:

◆ You can focus on the points that interest you most.

◆ You can go at your own pace.

◆ You can be completely relaxed and unashamedly honest in your answers to all the questions, since you don't have to share them with anyone!

Our suggestions for using this booklet on your own are these:

◆ Don't skip "Questions to Begin." The questions can help you as an individual reader warm up to the topic of the reading.

◆ Take your time on "Questions for Careful Reading" and "Questions for Application." While a group will probably not have enough time to work on all the questions, you can allow yourself the time to consider all of them if you are using the booklet by yourself.

◆ After reading the "Guide to the Reading," go back and reread the Scripture text before answering the "Questions for Application."

◆ Take the time to look up all the parenthetical Scripture references.

◆ Read the entire section of John's Gospel from chapter 11 through chapter 21, not just the parts excerpted in this booklet. Your total understanding of John's Gospel will be increased by reading through the entire second half.

◆ Since you control the pace, give yourself plenty of opportunities to reflect on the meaning of the Gospel for you. Let your reading be an opportunity for these words to become God's words to you.

Bibles

The following editions of the Bible contain the full set of biblical books recognized by the Catholic Church, along with a great deal of useful explanatory material:

◆ The Catholic Study Bible (Oxford University Press), which uses the text of the New American Bible
◆ The Catholic Bible: Personal Study Edition (Oxford University Press), which also uses the text of the New American Bible
◆ The New Jerusalem Bible, the regular (not the reader's) edition (Doubleday)

Books

◆ George R. Beasley-Murray, *John,* Word Biblical Commentary, vol. 36, 2nd ed. (Nashville: Thomas Nelson Publishers, 1999).
◆ Raymond E. Brown, S.S., *The Gospel according to John (XIII–XXI)* The Anchor Bible, vol. 29A (New York: Doubleday, 1970).
◆ St. John Chrysostom, *Commentary on Saint John the Apostle and Evangelist,* Homilies 44–88, Fathers of the Church, vol. 41, trans. Sister Thomas Aquinas Goggin, S.C.H. (New York: Fathers of the Church, Inc., 1960).
◆ Francis J. Moloney, S.D.B., *The Gospel of John,* Sacra Pagina Series, vol. 4 (Collegeville, Minn.: The Liturgical Press, 1998).
◆ Ben Witherington III, *John's Wisdom: A Commentary on the Fourth Gospel* (Louisville, Ky.: Westminster John Knox Press, 1995).

How has Scripture had an impact on your life? Was this book helpful to you in your study of the Bible? Please send comments, suggestions, and personal experiences to Kevin Perrotta, General Editor, Trade Editorial Department, Loyola Press, 3441 N. Ashland Ave., Chicago, IL 60657.